Vic Flick Guitarman
From James Bond to The Beatles and Beyond

For more information on Vic Flick and his CD, "James Bond Now,"
visit *www.vicflick.com*

Vic Flick: Guitarman
©2008 Vic Flick. All Rights Reserved.
No part of this book may be reproduced in any form or by any means, electronic, mechanical, digital, photocopying or recording, except for the inclusion in a review, without permission in writing from the publisher.

Published in the USA by:
BearManor Media
P O Box 71426
Albany, Georgia 31708
www.bearmanormedia.com

ISBN 978-1-59393-308-1

Printed in the United States of America.
Cover photograph by Neils Zlozwer.
Book design by Brian Pearce.

Table of Contents

Foreword 5
Introduction 7
The Beginning 9
Music Full Time 15
Drumbeat 25
Stringbeat 31
The Wheel Barrow 41
Concerts 45
Studios 63
Recording Sessions 87
Home Life 111
The Cruise 115
Dance Bands 119
The Bond Connection 121
The Beatles Connection 131
Among the Girls 137
Musicians 145
More Television 163
Musicians' Union 173
Coda 181
Equipment 185
Index 187

Dedicated to our daughter, Jayne Marie.

My very special thanks to my wife, Judy, and our son, Kevin for their encouragement and patience.

Foreword

I knew from the age of about eight that I would play the guitar, and I seemed to have been aware of Vic Flick all the time when I was growing up. In reality, I suppose it was *Drumbeat* that permanently fixed his image and sound in my mind. Buddy Holly was my inspiration, but Vic was final, absolute confirmation of my destiny. There were a number of reasons for that. Here are just a few of them...

His fabulous sound, not just on the low strings or the high (most famous guitar players of that time were identified by their style in one range only). He sounded great from the bottom E to the very top D.

He was a musician's musician. He played for all the greats, and on so many treasured recordings. *He* was in demand, and he delivered.

He looked fantastic with the guitar, and he looked great on TV (and he had great hair; I went out and tried to get mine to go the same!)

He always stood up to play! Yes, I know it sounds obvious – but you couldn't play 'our' music sitting down. The real guitar heroes always stood.

Everyone in school liked Vic Flick; we all had our favourite singers and would support them to the end, but Vic was the 'image' of The John Barry Seven to most of us and everyone had to own up that they were brilliant – and British.

His presence and sound with them, along with my other idols, The Shadows, who were just beginning to emerge, decided for me that the way to go forward was as part of a group, and I'm eternally grateful for that moment of realization.

Yes he was the man, and yes – he turned me on!

Justin Hayward,
The Moody Blues

Introduction

Dear Reader,

You're holding in your hands the autobiography of Vic Flick, one of the greatest studio musicians of a generation, if not of all time. This story is from "the horse's mouth" and not second-hand opinions from speculators who were not there when these incredible events and recordings actually happened.

As recording studios and record companies began to dominate the entertainment industry, songs had to be recorded quickly, efficiently, perfectly - and with feeling. It is easy to see why a vocal group, or a single vocalist, required a band. But why did famous groups need to be augmented, or even replaced?

In the '50s and especially the '60s, when bands came to dominate the youth market, the ones who came to fame did so because they had "the look" and "the sound." But performing well in a live situation does not necessarily make for efficient recording artists. For that reason, plus the fact that, especially in England, recording sessions were booked in three-hour segments (especially at the famous EMI Studios), generally from 10 a.m. – 1 p.m., 2:30 – 5:30 p.m. and again from 7 – 10 p.m. Besides reasons of economy and efficiency, this also allowed session musicians to travel from studio to studio to studio, with time to set up their gear, be properly miked, break down their equipment and travel to the next session.

With only some exceptions, young performing bands were not generally able to churn out up to five songs, often previously unheard, in this three-hour time span. Hence, producers often called upon the studio musicians. Sometimes an entire band was replaced on record, and sometimes only certain musicians. This generally does not reflect upon our chart-topping heroes' proficiency as musicians or performers, but only as recording artists.

Vic was one of a handful of first-call guitarists in London in the late '50s, '60s and '70s — an elite set including "Big" Jim Sullivan and "Little" Jimmy Page. Often, the guitarists would play in tandem, and sometimes as the sole guitarist, depending upon the arrangement.

Vic and I (and his lovely wife, Judy) have been friends for many years now, and I am humbled to write the introduction to this special and important book that has been in the making for so long. I had the pleasure and honor of playing on stage in Las Vegas with Vic, and words cannot describe the intensely sweet sounds of Vic's guitar coming directly from the amplifier that was only yards away from me. I watched him play and heard the sounds live and first-hand, and it was only then that I really understood.

You are in for a great treat. You are about to read first-hand accounts of the sounds behind "Swingin' London," and first-hand accounts of encounters with some of the greatest British, American and world-wide recording artists that provided the sound-track for our generation. Don't expect too much "dish" — as Vic, the consummate gentleman, has advised me: "If they're alive, take a dive. If they're dead, go ahead!" But don't expect an overly technical and even dull story, either. This book is riveting and incredibly insightful. Suspend what you think you know and read the truth in Vic Flick's incredible autobiography. I can promise you it will be like music.

Bob Rush

Bob Rush is the former musical director and bassist of a group called The Rip Chords, who had a huge U.S. hit record in 1964 with "Hey Little Cobra." The original group disbanded and Bob organized its reformation with, amongst others, two of the three original members. His interest in the '60s music sparked our friendship years ago and has been a great encouragement to me during the writing process, and a great deal to do with having my "Bond" guitar exhibited in the Rock and Roll Hall of Fame Museum. He has since left the Rip Chords and continues to be a Doctor of Chiropractic Medicine in Philadelphia, PA, in the US. He resides in Bucks County, PA with his wife and children.

The Beginning

The year was 1937 with World War II just a fleeting two years away. A terrible late winter storm ravaged the southern counties of England. The winds roared and howled with unimaginable might. The rain attacked the roofs, washed down the windows and beat the very Earth itself with the sound of a thousand crazed drummers. Inside the small room the light from a dim lamp forced its way through the misted window to the turmoil outside. The window, misted from the two buckets of steaming hot water on the hard stone floor, barely kept the elements from the small room. The gaunt features of a Midwife were softened by the lamp's orange glow — her starched cap shining white in contrast as she sat patiently by the humble bed. Waiting. Waiting. After what seemed hours, a legend was born.

Me!

Well, not quite. Actually, the morning of May 14th, 1937 was bright and sunny and I came screaming into the world with all the intent and purpose of one who was set to lead, or at least, make a lot of noise. My father, Harold, was a teacher, specializing in music and played the piano, and my mother, Mabel, was an accomplished singer. I fortunately carried their talents into the world. As you will have gathered from the rhetoric in the above paragraph, neither of them were writers. Still, I will try to defy genetics and share with you my story as a musician who had the good luck to make something of a name for himself in the years to come.

Before some fame and varying fortunes, I lived all my first eighteen years in Worcester Park, Surrey, England, and did all the things a boy was supposed to do — going to school, fighting, scrumping (purloining fruit from other peoples' back yards), dating girls and, from the age of fourteen, playing guitar. Earlier, my father insisted that I learn a musical instrument so, from the ages of five to twelve, I had piano lessons, and on a couple of occasions, violin lessons. I didn't take to the violin at all. This was possibly caused by the violin teacher who was at best a horrible person and at worst a dreadful teacher.

Even the violin teacher pales into insignificance compared to the experiences that I had from the age of two to seven, or maybe eight. Sometimes, following an air raid over London, my brother Alan and I would wake up on the floor of the hallway, outside the kitchen and dining room doors. That location surrounded by brick inner walls was deemed to be the safest and strongest place in the house for us to sleep. Consequently, we were awakened by parents and neighbors stepping over us holding slices of bread and cups of tea — always a cup of tea. It didn't seem to matter if the German bombs had blown up the water mains, cut the electricity, broken the gas mains and smashed all the cups in the house, there was always the miracle of a 'nice cup of tea.' When the 'all clear' siren had sounded we would go outside and look at the piles of smoking rubble that yesterday were houses, our friends' house. Perhaps a couple of ambulances parked alongside with maybe a few wardens picking through the rubble for signs of life. There was none. Not even the children I was supposed to go to school with that day.

The Government supplied us with a Morrison Shelter, a steel structure about three feet high, where the family could sleep under and run to when an air raid siren sounded. One night we were awakened from our sleep in this shelter by a stick of bombs dropping about our neighbourhood, and the resulting sound of splintering wood and shattering glass. When the 'all clear' sounded, we crept from our shelter to see the French Windows bowed in toward us and shards of glass, like darts, stuck in the mattress my father always placed facing the windows.

Bombs would shake the whole house. Ceilings would come down. Plates, cups and vases would fall from cupboards. It was like a continuous rumbling earthquake lasting for years — all with the background of anti-aircraft guns booming in the distance. The red glow of London burning in the far distance was a constant reminder of the conflict.

On the way to school I would find the spoils of war, remnants of the aerial dog fights between the Royal Air force and the Luftwaffa played out in the skies above London and its suburbs. Airman's boots, one with a foot in it and the leg bone sticking from it, pieces of airplanes, a spattering of shell cases. What an education for a child. Our teachers made us put all our small finds in a big box for collection by the war effort. Even then, recycling was the thing to do. At the height of the blitz we were evacuated to areas outside London to avoid the bombs. My family was sent to an English south coast town called Lancing. Even there we were not safe, as the cowardly German pilots would drop any remaining bombs on whatever they thought was a town as they scuttled back to Germany.

With this continuing danger, we were transported back to our home. Again, a few months later, I was 'evacuated' to my aunt's house about twenty miles west of London. At that time, Mr Hitler had developed the

V2 rocket, a winged bomb with a large jet engine attached. These instruments of death were very erratic in flight with a tendency to wander miles from their intended destination, the center of London.

One sunny day my cousin and I were stood outside my aunt's front gate when, sure enough, over the horizon came this dreadful weapon — heading straight for us. The rocket motor stopped its roar. The rocket now had to glide over a big field full of golden corn. With the thermals from the field, the rocket's right wing lifted and it turned away from us to disappear over a stand of trees. I can remember seeing the bolts holding the thing together — words — German words — and the red hot tip of the rocket. The resulting blast as the rocket landed on a Military hospital seemed to crush our ribs and stomachs. God knows what it must have been like when one of those things landed really close to you.

Everyone was on a strict diet due to rationing. A family of four had to subsist on something like eight ounces of bacon for a month. My father bred rabbits in an effort to give us meat. A vegetable garden took the place of my father's lawn. A chicken-wire enclosure at the bottom of our garden kept a couple of chickens and a few ducks, again for their meat and eggs. Candies were rationed, so we would look with longing at the rows of bottles in the Sweet Shop. Pig bins were supplied for any unused food to be saved. Pigs would eat anything — and the army needed bacon. Much to my father's dismay, the decorative chains linking posts on our front garden were cut down and used for tanks or bullets or anything warlike.

After the war, things slowly settled down, and a hesitant normality reigned.

When I was fourteen, my father and a friend from a few houses up the street formed a band to play at local church and political functions. My brother played the bass on an old cello that just seemed to appear from nowhere and, if I was to be in the band, I had to find an instrument to play. A guitar was advertised for sale in the local newspaper shop. A deal was struck and as a result I became the proud owner of a Gibson Kalamazoo, a small-bodied acoustic guitar. I practiced the instrument until the tips of my fingers bled. I had to catch up with all the others who were, compared to me, accomplished musicians. Slowly I improved, and moved from studying the Eddie Lang guitar tutor, page one, to getting through 'I'm in the Mood for Love' with only a couple of mistakes. Of course, with the volume of the other instruments, my valiant efforts went unnoticed. I fixed a Tank Commander's throat microphone to the machine head of my guitar and wired the cord into the back of my father's trusty radio. It worked. Looking back, the sound was not quite what was expected from a guitar, but at least I could be heard over the rest of the band.

Alan and I listened to a lot of jazz recordings. We tried starting a collection of different bands and musicians but that idea fell by the wayside when the cost of the 78s became prohibitive. I remember Gene Krupa, Artie Shaw, Charlie Christian, Mick Mulligan. Jim Hall and Joe Pass were also great inspirations. In an interview, Jim Hall argued he was not a guitarist but a song writer. I don't know any of his songs but they must be wonderful.

Tal Farlow is a great American guitarist who greatly influenced my playing and my desire to learn. His jazz lines, his chords and rhythmic comping all sustained my interest in the guitar when practice, which not only made perfect, but hurt and, dare I say it, became boring. Many years later Tal Farlow visited the UK for a few workshops and I was first in line for a seat. Sitting in the front row an Oriental gentleman sitting next to me asked to look at my camera. It was a good one and I proudly passed it to him. He was very interested and, I wrongly presumed, knowledgeable about cameras. After looking at the lense and thoroughly examining the camera, he handed it back to me. Later I met with and took photographs of Tal Farlow. Can you imagine my disappointment when the film was developed and was *blank*? The idiot Oriental had not replaced the lens correctly and the camera was rendered useless. I would have loved to have shared those pictures with you.

I left Kingston Grammar School in 1953 at the age of sixteen. Although scheduled to move into the 'Sixth Form,' one look at the academic requirements and the curriculum forced me out into the thriving work place. Barclays Bank welcomed me with open arms and, after nine months, those same arms threw me back into the thriving work place where I became a heating and ventilating technician. In my junior capacity this involved getting up at some ungodly hour, catching the first bus of the day and moving vast amounts of steel pipes, welding gear, dissolved acetylene and oxygen bottles around a wet, cold and muddy building site. These exertions prompted me to become a welder, which I became, and worked at the Fueling Depot of the Royal Navy in Rosyth, Scotland, for a company named Brightside Limited. Apart from drinking under age at the local Working Men's Clubs, the Company's name was the only bright thing about that little excursion. I then became the sing-along pianist on the nights the 'paid band' wasn't there. Not allowed to take money, the top of the piano finished up lined with pints of the finest Scottish ale, ale I felt obligated to drink. Consequently, those evenings are now shrouded in mystery. As that fine actor, Richard Harris, is quoted as having said; 'my drinking years were the most enjoyable I've known. Trouble is — I can't remember any of them!'

After the welding job, (which I must admit, I did enjoy), came Decca Radar and Navigator, with me employed as a wireman. Simply put, a wireman wired. All I did was wire up the valve bases on Naval radar sets and pass them to the next person for him or her to wire up something else. I was happy as I could do this in my sleep, which most days, I needed!

One day, management decided to evaluate their work force and distributed forms to be filled in. I put down what education I had and my ambitions and returned the form. Next thing I knew, an army of white coats clutching clip boards descended on my work place. Questions about the answers I had given flowed freely from this gaggle of middle-management persons. It was decided that I should be a draughtsman and my workplace changed overnight from the work bench to a brightly lit room full of men bent double over drawing boards with pencils and rulers. I didn't like it, but I was earning a pound a week more. All this time, I was playing gigs of varying sorts so requests from the section boss for me to start studying fell on stony ground.

Music Full Time

My first professional job on guitar was at a summer camp with a group of forward-looking musicians led by a musical maniac. This transition came about for me when I answered an advert in *The Melody Maker* for a guitar player at one of Butlins Holiday Camps — a kind of cold and wet Club Med with hard beds, bad food and warm beer. Les Clark was an extrovert character who played bass like a man possessed and ingested an amazing amount of Purple Hearts, Benzedrine and any other substance that would 'keep him going.' Les Clark interviewed and auditioned me over the phone by asking if I knew any tunes. I replied that I did, and reeled of a list of titles that naturally included 'I'm in the Mood for Love'.

'Great,' Les Clark said. 'See you at Skegness in April.'

I now had to give notice at my present job, a modifications draughtsman at Decca Radar and Navigator. Giving notice was made easier by the fact my boss and I were not on the best of terms. He had taken exception to me sleeping on my drawing board on a Monday morning after a particularly grueling Thursday, Friday, Saturday and Sunday playing guitar at dances, weddings and parties. When I actually told my boss (I'll always remember his name, Mr. Brautigan), he was, for the first time, speechless when I said I would be earning three times as much as a guitar player than I was as a draughtsman – and probably the amount he was earning after years of service at Decca. Of course, he could look forward to his pension as compensation.

Arriving at Butlins, I discovered I knew more tunes and more about music than any of the other musicians. Somehow, after a few rehearsals, Les Clark got this disparate bunch of people into some semblance of a band and our nightly performances began at the Rock and Calypso Ballroom. Billed as 'Les Clark and his Musical Maniacs,' we did some crazy things. I even learned I could play the guitar hanging upside-down by my legs behind an upright piano. These musical gymnastics took place when we did our twice-weekly 'concert' stint in the Camp Bar. Of course, the beer flowed and, maybe driven on by our exciting music, the crowd could get a bit rowdy. Once, whilst hanging upside down, I witnessed a man being hit on the head with a bar stool. The man collapsed in a heap, and whilst he was discreetly removed, the drinking and the music and my uncomfortable slant on life continued. We turned every tune we could think of into rock numbers — even 'My Bonnie Lies over the Ocean.' The kids loved it!

Occasionally, rival gangs from London would mistakenly book the same week for their holidays. This led to some pretty traumatic events that always seemed to happen in the Rock and Calypso Ballroom. One night a really serious fight started. The two warring factions seemed to roll across the seating in a mass of fists, swear words and blood. One luckless warrior was thrown through the air, upside down, cracking his nose and the front of his face on the edge of the stage, right in front of me. Up to that moment Les Clark had been shouting, 'Keep playing! Keep playing!' When the bits of bone and blood spattered me and my guitar, I was — in the words of the great prophet — 'Out a' there'. The band ran for the side of the stage heading for the safety of the dressing room — well — dressing *box*. For the security of our instruments between sessions, Butlins had supplied a small 6' by 6' box-type room. As small as it was, we were glad to hide there, listening to the bangs and crashes of the debacle taking place outside.

With occasional incidents (fortunately none as bad as the one I just described), the season came and went and I found myself back in London and on the dole. The few paying jobs I had were not enough to keep me in rent and food so I needed a little extra. My brother, Alan, played the tenor sax and violin and had the same desire to 'turn pro,' so we formed a band called The Vic Alan Quintet. We played a few gigs and did an audition for the Eric Winston Agency at the beginning of 1958. Alan had been a member of the RAF Dance Band based at Stanmore in the County of Middlesex and got the taste for the big band. So when an offer came from Sonny Swan, a famous dance band leader of the time, to join his sixteen-piece band in Bridlington (a northern beach side town), he took it. A few short days after he had signed the contract, Eric Winston 'phoned and offered us the job as the Rock and Roll band in Butlins at Clacton. At the audition I had thought it unusual that Eric was more interested in the fact I could read music than he was in the actual band. All was revealed in a 'phone call when he asked if I would play in his band at the Camp when he did his weekly BBC broadcast. Wow! My first shot at broadcasting.

Yes, of course I would!

I first met Les Reed in the autumn of 1957 at a pub called the Blackamores Head, located in Chessington, not far from the zoo in West London. The Blackamores Head had made a name for itself as a place for jazz in the evenings and a 'sing-song' on Sunday mornings. People used to come from miles around to sing at this pub, most of them because it was the only place in which they sounded good. What they didn't realize was that Les, on the piano, had perfect pitch, so, whenever our budding Frank Sinatras would wander out of key, Les used to follow them. 'He's the only pianist I can sing with,' these songsters would say as they lined up at the side of the small stage.

Les Reed and Vic. Clacton, 1958

However, the musicians that were gathered on stage wanted to play more than fifteen versions of 'I'm in the Mood for Love.' Not that 'Mood for Love' wasn't a great tune, but you can have too much of a good thing. I was sick of the song by now, anyway. To play more musically stimulating tunes, we would ignore the hopefuls and start one of our tunes before the singer could start organizing his moment of stardom. And organize it they would! Some would stipulate the tempo and key their song had to be in (not that it always mattered). Others would dictate the arrangement, how many choruses, when the trumpet should play, etcetera, and proceed to swallow the microphone in an effort to give an 'intimate' performance.

The Vic Alan Quintet was up and running – unfortunately, without Alan. He had signed on the dotted line and was now incarcerated on the Bridlington Promenade with Sonny Swan. So, into Clacton I went with Les Reed on piano, Bruce Gaylord on drums, Dave Green on tenor sax and flute and Jimmy Curry on bass. I made my first and last attempt at singing with such songs as 'Whole Lotta Woman' and 'Jailhouse Rock.' The group specialized in extra-long versions of popular instrumentals. 'Tom Hark' and 'Tequila' went on until desperation showed in the eyes of the dancers.

Downstairs from the Rock and Calypso Ballroom was the South Seas Coffee Bar. (I think Billy Butlin had a mental hang-up about tropical names). While I was upstairs in the Rock and Calypso Ballroom, performing in that Coffee bar downstairs was a very young Cliff Richard accompanied by his group the Drifters. He used to be there doing an imitation of Elvis most evenings and lunch times. Some afternoons you could find Cliff in the indoor swimming pool area singing to his own guitar. (The echo made him sound good!) As a precursor to his fame, Cliff was always surrounded by a bevy of young ladies, 'oohing' and 'aahing' as he worked through his swimming pool repertoire. He and the Drifters were subsequently moved from the Coffee Bar to the Pig and Whistle Pub due to the group's loud and over-enthusiastic performances. His music was thought by the management to be a better fit for the rowdy beer-swilling types than the genteel tea-and- coffee drinkers.

One day Cliff was jumping about, all excited. He was going to London to record a couple of songs and had permission from the Camp Commandant (Sorry, make that *Manager*) to be absent for two days. In an obvious attempt to dampen his enthusiasm, he had to make up the lost time with extra performances. They don't give anything away at those places!

One of the songs he recorded was a Sammy Samwell song called 'Move It,' for which he received (rumour has it) the princely sum of 20 pounds. I just hope Sammy wasn't ripped off like Cliff. Cliff's recording manager, Norrie Paramour, quickly signed him up to ensure his future income. (Norrie's that is, not Cliff's!) Norrie became know affectionately in the business as 'B-Side Norrie.' I suspect that very few of his artists' records were released without one of Norrie's tunes on the flip side. Good luck to him.

So, Cliff's life changed for the better and my life improved considerably, for it was at that Holiday Camp that I met Judy. We were married in the merry month of May, 1960. The next year our son Kevin Victor was born and, in 1964, along came Jayne Marie.

Returning to London from Clacton, my many contacts kept me quite busy and things in general took off like a rocket. The broadcasts with Eric Winston continued and there were a few concerts where he needed a guitar. It was during this time that I met George Jennings, a wonderful man, who played bass and was running a jazz club in a pub in the Isleworth district of London. George was also the bassist in a successful Skiffle group run by Bob Cort. Bearded and energetic, Bob was an advertising executive by day and a skiffler by night. Ken Sykora was one of the guitarists. By contrast, Ken's day job was announcer and producer for the BBC. The other guitarist in the group was Diz Dizley, a lovable character and a wonderful player in the Django Reinhardt style. I met Diz in the Charring Cross Road one day carrying his trusty guitar, the Clifford Essex Paragon De Luxe. Diz was selling this guitar due to pressing financial needs and we settled on the price of 40 pounds - a lot of money in those days. I'm sure Diz will be pleased to know that guitar made its place in musical history playing the 'James Bond Theme' and is now in the Rock and Roll Hall of Fame.

One night, at this pub in Isleworth, West London, George turned up with a pile of Bob Cort records and told me to go home and learn them. Ken was leaving the group to concentrate on his career at the BBC and George had put me up for the now-vacant position. Bob Cort was amazed at my audition when I played along as if I had been with the group forever - even playing Ken's guitar solos note for note. Skiffle had become an overnight sensation with artists such as Chas McDevitt and Nancy Whisky becoming household names. Bob Cort was cashing in on this phenomenon and had a series of records in the charts. Due to these hit records, Bob was offered a job on the bill with Paul Anka's first European tour. Anka's hit, 'Diana', had taken Britain by storm so this nationwide tour had been set up. Very exciting stuff. Also on the bill, and backing Paul Anka, was The John Barry Seven.

Restaurants in the towns of Great Britain, and especially the Northern towns, during the early 1960s were few and far between. Consequently, when everyone arrived in town for one of the Paul Anka concerts, and after finding digs, finding food was next on the list. John Barry and I found ourselves looking for the more exotic food, Indian or Chinese. That type of food was just beginning to catch on in Britain and the restaurants had to prove to the populace that the food was good. However, the really authentic Indian or Chinese food was not always palatable to the British. Those chefs who struck the happy medium were the most successful. I remember we found an excellent Chinese restaurant in downtown Manchester. The food and service were great. Later we learned that the owner of that restaurant was the person who supplied the whole of Britain with food and staff, even restaurant design. He was the first Chicken Chow Mein millionaire in Britain — and suitably inscrutable.

A moment of humor springs to mind. One of the dates on the Anka tour was Edinburgh, in Scotland. In order that our faces didn't look like white blobs on stage in the glare of the lights, we wore makeup, 'Pancake 28,' which gave us an instant tan. We then accented our eyebrows with eyeliner. At the very first chance we got, George and I headed for the nearest pub. Sitting at the bar, we got some strange looks from the regulars. Soon, with the aid of the local libation, remarks such as 'Bloody poufters', and 'They're letting anybody in here now,' became very audible.

George, who was at least six-foot-three-inches tall and 280 pounds, suddenly lost his cool. Picking one of the more loquacious drinkers up by the front of his shirt, he asked in a very intimidating voice: 'Who are you calling a fucking queer, you little Scotch shit!' With his feet dangling some six inches of the ground, our poor unfortunate was in no position to run, or do anything. His friends suddenly found other places they wanted to be. After being slowly lowered to the floor, our 'Mr Mouth' disappeared very quickly and we returned to our pints.

At the time, I was living with my parents in Worcester Park, Surrey. My father, a teacher, was wonderfully supportive of my music once he realized that was what I wanted to do. He did get worried when blank pages appeared in my diary. Even later, when I was doing as many sessions as the human body could do, he would express concern that I only had three weeks work in the book. 'You've got a wife, two kids and this big house to keep going on three weeks work. How are you going to do it?' he would constantly ask. Being a teacher, working for the government and looking forward to a pension, he couldn't grasp the freelance mindset at all. My mother was always supportive and even if she had concerns about my prospects, she never mentioned them. God blessed me with the best parents a person could wish for, parents who were always there when I needed them.

One day my Mother called me to the phone. 'It's someone called John Barry for you. He sounds very northern.' Of course he did; he was from Fulford, a suburb of York.

'I need you to join the band, Vic.' John said. 'There is the prospect of a lot of work and I need musicians who are good and can read.'

How could I turn down such an offer? After all, there was nothing else like this to look forward to. Meeting with John a few days later he explained the set up and gave me the guitar parts for a twenty-minute act. The John Barry Seven were to perform at the Metropolitan, Edgeware Road, London, in ten days' time.

'You need a band uniform. You need to learn these parts and you need to be at the rehearsal in two days,' John said.

'Yes,' I said. (What else was there to say?)

The rehearsal was held in a basement under a restaurant in Soho. I recall making my way down some stairs to a dimly lit area. I had met most of the other musicians on the Paul Anka tour, but I was there to take the place of a long time member so I was greeted somewhat warily and coldly by the rest of the band. Rehearsal went fine, helping to break down the cool attitude of the guys. The other guitarist, Keith Kelly, was a good rhythm guitar player but had delusions of being a solo act, playing guitar and singing à la Buddy Holly. John Barry told everybody how crucial this appearance at the Metropolitan was to the future of the band. This didn't do much for my blood pressure — as young as I was. Eve Taylor, our manager, had made the booking and invited as many critics, agents, directors and producers as she could. It seemed like everyone's career was hanging on my performance. I have had some nerve-wracking experiences in my time but this one ranks with the best, or worst, depending on which way you look at it.

'Variety' was still alive and kicking so the auditorium at the Metropolitan was full. I can remember standing at the back of the audience during the first half, enjoying the excitement and atmosphere in this old theater. I leaned against the ornate woodwork of the Stalls Bar and tried to picture all the vaudeville artistes who had performed there. The John Barry Seven was scheduled to go on after the interval so there was plenty of time to set up behind the curtain. There was also plenty of time to get good and nervous. Every note that I had committed to memory had vaporized from my mind. I stared at the curtain, my stomach churning, my lips dry and my forehead damp with a cold sweat. Why was I doing this to myself? All those previous jobs — bank clerk, welder, wireman and draughtsman — took on an attraction I had never realized before. In fact, at that moment, I started to wish I was five years old and could start all over again.

'Mummy, Mummy, where are you?'

As the house lights dimmed and the stagehands prepared to walk the curtain back, I heard an echoing announcement: 'Ladies and Gentlemen, The John Barry Seven.' Those words seemed to float around in my head as the curtains parted and the expectant applause rose from the darkness. Two incredibly bright spotlights played on the stage, semi-blinding me. Suddenly John's dour northern voice cut through the haze with: 'One, two, one, two, three, four.'

My fingers clasped the guitar neck and somehow the opening chords of 'Bees Knees' resounded from my amplifier. It was a struggle to keep moving about, smiling and remembering the music and my performance wasn't (to me) note perfect, but at the end John congratulated us all.

I had just entered a new phase of my life.

From what seemed, in retrospect, the sedate, ordered existence of my suburban life with jazz clubs, weddings and dances, I was thrown into a succession of concerts, broadcasts, television, photographic sessions and all the necessities of 'Show Biz.' There were very few television productions for bands to appear on and one of those was the prestigious

'Jack Jackson Show.' Situated in a small underground studio in London, the show featured host Jack Jackson and a singer by the name of Glen Mason. The Seven appeared several times on this show, either to promote our latest record or just to make an appearance. The abundance of work that John Barry had predicted was certainly being realized.

John Barry Seven with Keith (Buddy Holly) Kelly on rhythm guitar.

Les Reed and I were sharing a flat in Nottinghill Gate with another musician, drummer Dick Harwood. Eve Taylor had got word the BBC were to run a Pop Music style program similar to ITV's *Oh Boy*. To prepare for an audition that had been arranged with the future Director of *Drumbeat*, three things happened. Because he couldn't read music and because he wanted to carve a solo career for himself, Keith Kelly left the band. John Barry needed a pianist to cover any keyboard parts for the TV show, and the band needed a new sound. I suggested my flat mate and friend for the job. A meeting was set up and Les Reed was hired on piano. At that time, Jennings Music had introduced the 'Piano Pick Up.' A contact microphone that was fitted inside a small block of wood and the whole contraption was taped or clamped to the sounding board of a piano. Connected to an amplifier, the volume and tone of the piano could be changed to suit the occasion. Add a tremolo effect to the output and you had 'The New Sound'!

BBC Television Producer and Director Stewart Morris had been commissioned to produce an upbeat, fast-paced pop music show in contrast to, and in competition with, Independent Television's *Oh Boy* and BBC's own *Dig This*. Eve Taylor had sold the idea of the Seven to Stewart with one of the selling points being, of course, 'The New Sound.' We had been rehearsing with Les to include the piano sounds into the arrangements and an audition was set for Stewart Morris to hear the band. We arrived at a pub in Shepherds Bush and set up our equipment. Everything was good except that there was no Les and no 'New Sound.' I had left the flat earlier than Les as a lot of the gear that needed setting up was in my car. Les was just waking up as I left. He'd had a gig that finished in the small hours of that morning so wasn't 'quite with it.'

A few moments before the appointed time, Stewart burst into the room with his assistant, Yvonne Littlewood, and as was his habit, wanted everything to start immediately. 'Hello, and where's the new sound?' Stewart demanded.

To this day I don't know what made me say, 'I think it's still in bed.'

The nervous laughter helped to lessen the impact of Les's entrance. Rushing through the door, trailing the wire from the pick up, Les apologized, stuck the pick up on the piano, plugged it into his amp and sat down with a sigh. Stewart and Yvonne took their seats at a table and got ready to listen. We played, and every note was an historic event. When we had finished, Stewart got up from his chair, walked toward us and in a rare moment of excessive praise said, 'Good. See you on the set.'

So, in 1959, we had entered the world of the Television Series. I have been involved with many series, but never one that was as innovative and exciting as this. Booked to be resident on the show were the John Barry Seven and Bob Miller and his Miller Men, a swinging eighteen-piece band. Colour television had not yet been perfected, a fact that didn't stop Stewart from 'putting on a show.' Each band had its own colour uniform. The Seven were pink and the Miller Men yellow, green and red. None of this spectacle could be seen by the viewers, but I'm sure it gave the TV picture light and shade and a perspective that was unique. What a pity, that to my knowledge, not one of the series was recorded. The big star to emerge from *Drumbeat* was Adam Faith. He had a couple of hit records and had appeared on *Oh Boy*, but it was *Drumbeat* that turned him into the Nation's favorite singer.

A 1966 *Crescendo* magazine advertisment for Hammond. That's me on guitar!

Drumbeat

Drumbeat was certainly a wonderful and exciting experience for me. Every week the John Barry Seven were rehearsing our solo band numbers, checking the backing for artists and working with the director with any camera movements that we might be involved in. I often worked with the Miller Men when Bryan Daly or Mike Morton couldn't make the date. I've included a picture taken from a 1966 *Crescendo Magazine* which shows me with the band in a television studio, the picture being used to advertise the Hammond Organ. Unfortunately, the organ hides the band's fine pianist, Gerry Butler.

One of the nicest people to appear fairly regularly on the show was Russ Conway. He was always very appreciative of the backing the John Barry Seven provided for him and we came to look forward to his appearances on the show. Russ was very nervous. If he could have overcome this affliction, he could have become a big international star. On one occasion, during camera rehearsal when Russ was promoting his latest release, either 'Roulette' or 'China Tea,' he became so nervous and unsure of himself that he actually stopped playing. On transmission, Les Reed had to play the same tune, off camera, as much in sync as possible in case Russ did stop playing. The cameras were ready to cut away to a long shot and the sound would feature Les's piano if Russ did goof up. Thankfully, all went well and the record went to the top of the charts. Maybe that was the start of 'the two-piano sound.' For an instrumentalist, Russ was phenomenally successful and popular, yet he never changed in his attitude towards those people fortunate enough to work with him — he was always warm and friendly. I played rhythm guitar on a couple of Russ's records and these were enjoyable experiences.

Another pianist on *Drumbeat* was Roy Young. Roy's specialty was doing rip-offs of Jerry Lee Lewis and Little Richard — and very good he was, too. He sang and played with the same complete abandon and enthusiasm as his idols. This excess of enthusiasm (coupled with Roy usually being positioned some distance from the backing group) made backing him a difficult and musically hazardous task. If the band got into

Roy Young and the John Barry Seven on *Drumbeat,* 1959.

The John Barry Seven on *Drumbeat.* From the left, Jimmy Stead, Dennis King, Dougie Wright, John Barry, Mike Peters, Vic Flick and Les Reed.

a groove then Roy would use this as a spring board to take off on a tangent. Musical chaos would be the result. These television broadcasts were long before the days when every musician had his/her own head set, so to avoid parting musical company with Roy, we had to listen like crazy and pick our way tenderly along behind him. This didn't always make for a roaring, stomping, Jerry Lee Lewis-type performance, but it was at least marginally correct.

The entire *Drumbeat* Cast: The John Barry Seven, Bob Miller and the Miller Men, Adam Faith, Roy Young, Vince Eager, Sylvia Sands and Danny Williams.

Then there were the Barry Sisters who were the British version of the Poni Tails; Vince Eager, a very good Elvis clone; Peter Gordeno, a brilliant dancer who insisted on singing; and The Raindrops—a two-boy, one-girl singing group. The girl was Jackie Lee and two guys were Len Beadle and Johnny Worth. Jackie went on to carve a successful solo career with a couple of hit records in the UK and Len became a Record Company executive with the obligatory suit and personality change. Johnny Worth, known as Les Vandyke amongst the songwriting community, penned many hits for Adam Faith and other artists, some with my old friend Les Reed.

Guitar Boogie Shuffle was a big hit for Bert Weedon in the UK in 1959 and it fell upon me to perform the number on the show. Stewart came over and asked me if I had a 60-foot-long cord (cable) for my guitar.

'Not on me,' I replied.

He wanted me right out in the center of the studio so the cameras could circle me, like Indians on the attack. He had a cord made up which, unfortunately, wasn't ready when we rehearsed it, so I stood in the middle and made faint clicking noises and listened to the John Barry group playing way over near the studio wall. Comes the show and the cord turns up.

Lights! Camera! Action!

There I was on the end of this 60-foot cord playing the first few bars on my own and hearing myself for what seemed like ten seconds after I had played. When the group came in, what little of my playing I could hear above their playing seemed totally out of sync. This situation was bad enough. Because of my nervousness at being so visually and musically exposed, I had started the number at a breakneck speed. What should have been a low 'E' played as quarter notes, the tempo that I set made them into eighth notes. Consequently, everything that followed was nearly twice as fast as it should have been. If you can recall 'Guitar Boogie Shuffle,' you will realize that's a hell of a lot of notes to play at twice the speed they were originally recorded at. That was one of the longest two minutes of my life — or was it just a minute? I just ploughed on, and the group just ploughed on, and the number collapsed to a crumbling finish. Don't forget that this debacle was going out live: 'No going back on this one, baby.'

It never pays to be too critical of one's own performance. For weeks after that show people would come up to me and say how much they enjoyed the 'Guitar Boogie' solo spot, and how good I was. I think the general public somehow listens through their eyes.

It was on another of this series that I went completely blank during the group's solo number. Maybe I was tired from the amount of work the band was doing. Maybe it was getting to me that every number the band did was a solo guitar number, but suddenly I had no more idea of what I had to play than flying to the moon. The number was 'Little John,' an arrangement by John Barry of an old sea shanty with several places where I played completely on my own. The key change was one of them. The rest of the guys were staring at me and either whistling or 'la la-ing' my part. Nothing registered. After a few seconds I returned to the real world, remembered where I was in the number and carried on. The big trouble was that Stewart Morris had all his camera shots locked into the measures of the music, and when nothing happened, the camera continuity was destroyed. I think the rest of the number was completed with a safe long shot! Outside the studio, John Barry threw one of his 'I'm the band leader' fits. He jumped up and down, his eyes bulging, shouting, 'Don't ever do that again!' Was I ever likely to?

There were technical problems, too. Stewart had the cameras rushing around the studio in a sometimes-futile attempt to make their next position. Part of the show's character came from the pace of the many camera shots. On one show the big 'dolly' that carried Camera Number 1 was racing across the studio floor to get to its next mark when there was a crackling sound, an enormous showering cascade of sparks and the 'dolly' came to a slow and uncontrolled halt. The protective bar that circled the base of the 'dolly' had been bent up just enough to let the 1 ½" cable loom that brought power to, and took signals from the camera and motors, slip under and be sliced through. Of course, panic broke out on the floor and in the control room. Stewart's voice could be heard screaming through the camera operator's headsets to 'Do something!' All the shots had to be rewritten on the fly and the show continued with just a few minor glitches. The crew did an amazing job keeping the show going considering the main camera was out of action. Ron Green, the No.1 cameraman who went on to be the BBC's chief cameraman, remained calm and collected throughout the incident; indeed, he was one of the reasons the show got back onto an even keel again. There were many other incidents throughout my career that Ron must have observed from atop the arm of the No.1 Camera dolly.

A lot of long-time friendships developed from that TV show. Bob Miller's pianist then and for many years was Gerry Butler, a brilliant musician, who was responsible for many of the show's arrangements and often very ably assisted by arranger Len Hunter. Gerry and I have worked together countless times since those early days. His music was always of the highest standard and I have always been flattered that he asked me to work on so many of his projects. An example of his piano technique was when a film company asked me to write a music track for an edited and processed black-and-white 'silent' movie for Channel 4 Television. I booked Gerry to play the solo piano part. Jon Hiseman was the engineer in his own studio, Temple Music Studios in Sutton, Surrey, and he sat and looked in wonder at the VU meters. Gerry's playing volume was so controlled and so even that there was no need to limit or even ride the fader. Many of the musicians from *Drumbeat* went on to be very well-known session players: guitarist Bryan Daly, drummers Andy White (of Beatle fame), Doug Wright, trumpeter Bobby Haughey, and pianist Les Reed, to name but a few.

During this momentous series a romance blossomed between the director, Stewart Morris and a singer named Sylvia Sands. Originally booked on an as-needed basis, towards the end of the series she never missed a show! Sylvia was a beautiful, tall, dark-haired girl who had passed an audition for the series as a singer of 'standards.' Young and inexperienced, she faced a daunting task having to compete with the many excellent singers who were around at the time. Her rendition of 'I've Got My Love to Keep Me Warm' was particularly memorable. The sixth bar of the melody runs up a diminished chord. Miss Sands would always get it confused with a major chord with the predictable conflicting results. Hearing she was wrong (and never understanding why), her intonation suffered in direct relationship with the ascent of the melody line. Never before or since have I seen twenty-five to thirty musicians cringe at the same time.

From the moment of her entry into show business, Sylvia was carefully chaperoned by her parents—at least, I think it was her parents. This constant vigil no doubt added an excess of spice to Sylvia's and Stewart's clandestine meetings, accelerating their passion enough for them to sporadically throw caution to the winds. Now and then one of the crew or the musicians would catch them in an embrace behind a set or holding hands in the car park. No one was supposed to know what was going on and any talk of the liaison was discreetly avoided on the set. It was all very lovely and romantic. They eventually got married — and eventually got divorced, and neither event was a surprise to anybody.

An episode that damped Stewart's ardor for a few moments concerned his beloved car. Parking space was limited and cramped at the BBC Television Centre which made maneuvering a perilous task. One day John Barry called for a meeting and, not up to the expertise required in the Centre's Car Park, he backed into Stewart's Jaguar. The damage was horrific for the slow speed at impact. Apparently, Barry's rear bumper had hit the twin exhausts of Stewart's car, forcing the whole assembly forward, bending the exhaust, cracking the manifold and committing Stewart to an expensive repair and a long time without his dream car. The parts needed were difficult to come by and the car was a long time out of action. I don't know how the matter was settled, but relations were icy for a couple of shows.

The *Drumbeat* studio was situated by the river Thames at Hammersmith. The restaurant looked out over the river and watching the water traffic during breaks made a picturesque change from the confinement of the studios and the road traffic we had to fight through on a daily basis. As with so many places I worked at, and have memories of, it has changed its use. It is now a storage and office facility.

Stringbeat

The recording of the album Stringbeat in 1961 was a major turning point in my career — in more ways than one! The big solo guitar sound was all the rage with hit records like 'The Peter Gunn Theme' and 'Shazam' in the charts. John Barry had long used my guitar as the featured instrument in his Seven recordings and was now determined to milk the commerciality of the sound to the full. Using the 'plus four' sound and a full-string section, we recorded Stringbeat in three sessions at EMI — EMI Studio 2, to be exact. EMI 2 has been photographed many times so I expect most people know that it is a big room (not as big as EMI 3, but still a big room).

Along the back wall was set the rhythm section, piano, bass and drums. Slightly in front of them was a lone chair and music stand. That was where I sat and performed for nine hours with just a few short breaks in between. Faced with a wall of violins, violas and cellos, I surveyed the pile of music in front of me. Turning page after page, it dawned on me that I was never going to stop playing solo guitar for the whole day. Interspersed with the written notes were such comments as 'Fill behind strings' or 'Adlib solo for 16 bars.' I was starting to realize that quite a lot depended on me for the making of this album. At that very moment, I didn't realize how much my future session career depended on my performance during that day. All the contractors, or fixers, in the recording industry at that time were violin players — and all of them were sitting in a row a few feet in front of me! Many of the string players, apart from those luckless violinists who had plucked there way to fame on the 'plus four' recordings, met my eyes with stony looks.

Guitarists today might listen to a copy of that album and find room for criticism. The sound of my guitar left a lot to be desired by modern standards. Sometimes the playing was not as accurate as even I would have liked, but I would challenge any one of them, under those circumstances and at that moment in time, to do better.

I think it was twelve or thirteen titles we recorded that day, all recorded onto compatible stereo. No tracking. No overdubbing. No, 'I'll put it on later.' The A&R man for those sessions was Norman Newell and his assistant was John Burgess. Both men went on to carve auspicious careers in the music business. Many years later I was working with John Burgess and we got to talking about 'those days.' John said something in that conversation that took me many, many days to get over. I don't think he realized what an effect it had on me. Even to this day I feel a little sick to my stomach when I recall what he said: 'Vic, it's a pity you were under contract to John Barry, because EMI wanted to make you their answer to Duane Eddy.'

'I was never under contract to John Barry,' I replied, my knees starting to go weak.

'That's what he told EMI when he was asked about you,' John stated.

As the ramifications of this sank in, anything else he said after that might as well have been in Hindu as far as I was concerned. I had only taken the position of 'leader of the band' out of, now it would seem, some misguided loyalty. There I was, chasing around the country, leading a sometimes disgruntled band of musicians, just to keep John Barry's name alive while he composed his film scores.

In August of 1963, when I left the band, I had given John Barry six months notice of my intentions. I had mentioned the approaching deadline many times in our conversations and two weeks prior to my last date in Torquay I reminded him again that I was leaving.

'What am I going to do? I haven't got anybody to take your place,' Barry said. 'Don't drop me in the shit.'

I might have stayed a little longer but my wife, Judy, told me in no uncertain terms to tell Barry that my decision was final.

After that long day recording Stringbeat, my telephone started to ring and sessions for other musical directors began to fill my diary. To complicate matters, John Barry decided to come off the road and concentrate on his film score writing. 'Would you lead the band?' he wanted to know.

In retrospect, I shouldn't have. By taking on this responsibility, not only was I putting stress on my life with all the extra sessions, TVs and broadcasts, but from my experience with leading a band at Butlins in the 50s I knew what crap I would have to take as a leader. There was a certain amount of animosity from some of the guys, but after a few weeks things calmed down and off on our tours we went. Every now and then a date would come up where the booker would insist on John Barry making a personal appearance with the Seven. I have to say that the music that we were playing, now that Barry wasn't directly involved wasn't as up to date as it could be. Barry was reluctant to pay for new arrangements. We had a few 'curtain raisers' that I placed throughout the program to keep things moving, but when he was there as a 'personal appearance,' he would pick all the best numbers for his moments on stage.

The Seven were part of the opening ceremonies for the enormous Silver Blades Ice Rink in Streatham, South London, and Barry made one of his very few 'personal appearances.' He called out the list of special numbers we were to do when he was on stage. 'That doesn't leave much for us to do for the rest of the night,' I said.

'That's OK,' Barry replied. 'I won't be here.'

Some of the skaters commented how much better the band was when John Barry played. Sometimes one has to bite one's tongue. Who played trumpet when Barry wasn't there, you might ask? Good question. I can't actually remember auditioning trumpet players for the vacant position, but on a recommendation, Bobby Carr was hired and stayed with the band for a couple of years. It spoke volumes for Barry's trumpet playing when Bobby, playing Barry's written parts, commented, 'I've never played rhythm trumpet before.' After three months, Bobby began to complain that he couldn't see himself getting a job in another band as his lip had gone. Playing nothing above 'C' in the treble clef all night didn't stretch Bobby's capabilities much at all. Still, as he said, the money keeps coming in and once you get used to it, it's difficult to give up.

There was some friction between members of the band, as there is in all walks of life. One night, just before we went on to play at a dance, a fight broke out between Bobby and Mike Peters, the bass player. Mike finished up tearing the shirt off Bobby's back and throwing it in the trash. If there was one thing Bobby didn't have a lot of it was shirts. It was a 'one off' gig so nobody had a spare white shirt. Bobby eventually appeared wearing a colored shirt that led everybody to think he was John Barry. This upset Mike even more as Bobby was getting all the attention. One night at the Leas Cliff Hall in Eastbourne, another fight broke out. Some horseplay started and Jimmy Stead, one of the Sax players, splashed some water, again, on Mike Peters. Mike filled a cup with water and threw it at Jimmy — most of it going over other guys in the dressing room. I'm not saying who it was, but someone picked up the fire bucket full of dirty stagnant water and managed to throw it over most of the band. Adding to the drama of the moment was amplified by the band being due on stage in about five minutes. There was the band, dripping with dirty water, swearing at each other and threatening to throw each other out the windows and down the cliff face and in the middle was John Barry doing, yet again, his jumping up and down 'I'm the bandleader bit' and shouting, yet again, 'I will disband. I will disband.'

I wish he had!

We got more than a few strange looks from the audience as a very quick 'make do' was done with the uniforms. Because Doug Wright's and Les Reed's trousers were hidden by the drums and piano respectively, their trousers were given to the front line troops. My trousers and Dennis King's were flapping above our ankles. Any colour shirt was allowed as most of the white ones were stained by the water — and playing an hour set in wet socks and underwear is not a pleasant thing to have to do.

Another moment of madness came in the good town of Burnley when the Seven played at, I think, the Mayor's Inaugural Ball. The big mistake the organizers made, at least from Mike Peter's point of view, was having a free bar set up behind the stage. Mike was going through some emotional traumas and was also very short of money. The free gin was soon pouring down Mike's thirsty throat in an effort to put the world back to rights. Mike managed to hold his own pretty well until right at the very end when, just before we played 'God Save the Queen,' his low 'E' string broke. Not only was it a very expensive string to replace, Mike didn't even have a replacement. He stopped playing and stared in disbelief at the flapping, useless string. He tore at it. He swore at it. He waved the bass around his head, threatening to throw it into the crowd. Following its gyrations with wild eyes, I shouted to Doug Wright: 'The Queen!'

Doug began the drum roll that started the Anthem. I surveyed the guys in the band. Their eyes were glued on Mike — as were the horrified eyes of the Mayor and most of the good people of Burnley. Just a few bars into the Anthem, Mike placed his useless bass so it rested at an angle with the raised drum rostrum. Running to the front of the stage, he turned and with a scream of 'Fuck it!' took a running leap at the offending instrument. Landing with both feet, the bass splintered into pieces and Mike disappeared off stage. The audience was transfixed, staring unbelievingly at the action that had just taken place. Les Reed was prostrate across the piano keyboard in a paralysis of laughter while the rest of the band came to the end of a bass-less and sped-up version of 'God Save The Queen.'

One of the Hall Officials had called for Security to go backstage and take control of Mike, who was now ranting and raving about his continuing bad luck. It was decided to remove him from the premises and he was frog-marched out the ballroom and down a long sloping and brass-railed flight of stairs. Demanding to be let loose by the two hefty security guards, Mike insisted in showing his strength to underline what he would do to the guards if they didn't let him go.

'See that brass rail,' he shrieked. 'Watch me break it like I'll break you if you don't get out a' my way.'

With this, Mike raised his right arm as high as it would go and with all the force he could muster, brought his fist down on the shining brass stair rail. There was a sickening crack and the colour drained from Mike's face. His wrist and his hand hung limp from the end of his arm. After being taken to hospital, Mike was declared seriously out of action, adding even further to his list of hardships. Various bass players were hired to fill his spot.

Remember what I said about being a band leader?

For many months we had been on to John Barry to either let us sing or get a singer. He would say, 'I started as an instrumental band and that's what it's going to be,' in answer to our pleas. One day, out of the blue, Barry announced we were going to have a singer — a girl singer. Lisa Page, the sister of Jill Day, joined the band and made not the slightest difference to the band's future or popularity. She had the personality of a three-day-old wet lettuce leaf and her singing left a lot to be desired, too. She reacted in a very negative manner with all the guys in the band and must have been the only girl singer with a band in musical history that nobody fancied. It's not that she wasn't pretty — she was, in a heavily made up way, but she had nothing to offer.

To give an example of how she went on, we were driving back from a gig up north in the middle of winter. Lisa was sat in the back with her handbag on her lap. She never let it out of her sight, even whilst she was onstage. I was driving and there were a couple of guys in the car with us. There were warnings of 'black ice.' This ice was the same colour as the road surface and very difficult to see, especially at the speed we normally traveled at. Speeding into Bawtry at about two in the morning, we hit our first patch of black ice and the car wandered a little before hitting dry road. Perhaps I relaxed a little after that because when we hit our second patch of black ice, I lost it. The car did circles, round and round down Bawtry High Street, much to the amazement and horror of a city worker who with shovel and sand was trying to beat the elements.

It's wonderful how peoples' expressions stay in your memory. To this day I can still see that worker's face as my car, lights blazing, gyrated past him on its way through town. I must have a guardian angel because, just as we were facing the right way, dry road once more appeared and with the car swaying as it regained its balance we were on our way to London. All of the guys began to cheer and swear as we thanked our lucky stars for still being in one piece. Lisa Page, on the other hand, had not moved one inch nor had her expression or the position of her handbag changed throughout the whole ordeal.

Touring had its discomforts, being away from the family, staying in strange 'digs' and always on the move, but there were compensations.

(I'll try and think of some by the end of this book!) Touring Ireland twice, once with John Barry and once without, was not without some humorous episodes. One of the strange things about playing Ireland was the ballrooms. You could travel for miles by car, along deserted winding roads, through unpopulated countryside and suddenly, in the middle of a field, be confronted by an enormous ballroom. Constructed of building blocks with a stage of nailed-together pallets, they seemed bleak places during the day. Where were the people supposed to come from? The place was deserted. We would unload our gear and set up then speed of to a hotel to wash up and eat, get changed and then return to the ballroom. The place was transformed. The fields all around were full of cars and trucks of all descriptions. Inside, the crowd was elbow to elbow and desperately fueling up for the evening's festivities.

And when the Irish dance, they dance. Starting at 9 p.m., the music was expected to go on till at least two in the morning. This scheduling didn't tally with the amount of music we had available. The 'house band' leader came up to me at one location and said, 'We'll start 'de dancin' at noin o'clock and you'se can come on at ten o'clock, and Good Luck to you, sor.'

'Just a minute,' I said, stopping him from returning to the bar. 'We go on at 10.30 p.m. till 11.30 p.m. and then from 12.30 a.m. to 1.30 a.m.'

With a look of profound disbelief on his rugged countenance, he said, 'You'se is 'de faymous ones, not us. You'se 'ave to play all night.'

With my eyes narrowing, actually from panic but which I hoped could pass for determination, I said, 'Not tonight, me old Mate. See you at 10.30.' I didn't mention that we were advertised outside the ballroom in letters four-feet high as 'The Jamboree Seven.'

The Irish tours were organized by Louis Rogers. Louis, the father of that charming lady and lovely singer, Clodagh Rogers, was a tall, elegant man, with a completely unflappable personality. Louis led us like a knight in shining armour through the pastures of Ireland, both north and south. A wonderful tale of Irish determination comes to mind. The driver and roady of our second tour was a fine gentleman by the name of Nuggy Mcgrath. Nuggy was built like an ox and exhibited the same personality traits if pushed too far. (Fortunately, we only saw the pleasant side of his character.) This particular tour took us to Kilarney where we stayed in a lovely Hotel beside the lake. The owner, a middle-aged lady, was very welcoming and made us feel very much at home. The hotel had a small landing stage where a sleek-looking motor boat was moored.

'Anybody want to go water skiing?' this lady asked.

We all declined, but Nuggy, not one to turn down a challenge, shouted. 'Oi'll do it!"

'The water is a tad bit cold,' the kind lady warned our hero.

'No matter. Show me how to do it,' he said, undaunted.

There followed a short tutoring where Nuggy was told to keep his arms straight at all times and let the boat take him — and not to fight the boat.

'OK! OK!' Nuggy said, his face glowing with enthusiasm.

Sitting on the edge of the dock with two large water skis strapped to his feet, you could almost hear him concentrating on keeping his arms straight.

'Ready?' the lady shouted.

'Go!' came the excited reply.

The motor boat sped off and Nuggy was whisked from the dry land and into the icy, still waters of the lake. With an Irish oath blurting from his mouth as he hit the water, Nuggy disappeared from view. All that could be seen was a small rooster's tail of water from the rope as it cut its way through the surface of the lake. Not a sign of Nuggy. The motor boat slowed to a halt and a concerned-looking lady surveyed the water behind her. We were now in hysterics. The line had gone slack. From the depths, one ski bobbed to the surface, followed closely by Neptune himself. There was Nuggy, spluttering and gasping for air and covered in weeds and other debris from the bottom of the lake. No attempt to rescue the struggling Nuggy was made by anyone. We were all too weak from laughter to do a thing. Clutching both skis, Nuggy made his way to the side of the lake and pulled himself onto the landing stage. With red eyes and a mud-covered face Nuggy said. "I don' like water skiing."

The Irish people are wonderful and I look forward to my next visit.

Back in England, several changes were happening within the ranks of the Seven. Les Reed decided to leave and further his composing and arranging career. Barry had used Les to help him with scoring and arranging and, I think, with some compositions. Through contacts he had made with the Seven, Les had an outlet for his songwriting talents, writing such hits as "It's Not Unusual' and 'Delilah' for Tom Jones and 'The Last Waltz' for Engelbert Humperdinck. (He wrote many more that I could mention but, Hey! It's my book.) Les wrote a lot with Barry Mason, a very talented and commercially orientated lyricist. I first met Barry Mason in 1956/7 when we used to do 'the American Camps' with Lee 'Bostick' Martin. There was an American saxophone player named Earl Martin who had a big instrumental hit with 'Flamingo.' Well, Lee modeled himself on Earl and used to play all night with this raucous, overblown tone.

Lee would hire a group of strippers and we would all set off in a rickety old bus for the wilds of Norfolk or some of the places where they had these American camps. Barry, being the vocalist, had place of honor in this old bus: a deck chair nailed to the floor. The rest of us would be on drum cases or kitchen chairs, hanging on for dear life until we got to our destination. There, the American Airman would be waiting for the entertainment we Brits were going to provide. The Airmen wanted to see the strippers as much as we wanted to sit down to a plate of their wonderful juicy T-Bone steaks, onion rings and a bucket of French fries. Such delights were impossible to come by in England. However, as the Yanks were paying, the Brits were playing, so we set up and got on with the show. I don't think any of the girls would have passed the audition for the Follies Bergere, but they were game old birds and were out there earning a bit of extra housekeeping.

We had to find a replacement for Mr Reed. Brian Hazelby filled the piano chair for a period of time. The Pop World and Pop music were very much below our Brian's standards, but because he had a mortgage and other sundry debts, he agreed to play with the band. He was a good pianist, and certainly the best that had been made available. That he was the only one certainly made choosing him easy. Every time we got to a gig, Brian would make for the piano and start practicing Chopin or Bach instead of helping with the gear. Someone nicknamed him 'Rachmaninoff' and it stuck to such an extent I had great difficulty in remembering his real name. But here was another Lisa Page situation in the making. I had to tell him to pull his weight, which he did to some measure, but always reluctantly. One concert on the North East Coast, Rachmaninoff came 'into his own.' When we got there we discovered, to our horror, that we were scheduled to do a two-hour concert. With a seated audience and just thirty minutes of concert type music, the threat of failure and ridicule loomed large.

I turned to Rachmaninoff and said, 'You know all those tunes you've been practicing?' I said, hopefully. 'Well, now is the time to perform them in concert!'

His little face lit up. 'Shall I go on first?' he asked, eagerly. Although I was happy to have so much cooperation, I was starting to think I had a tiger by its tail.

'The band will do a couple of numbers, then you can announce your selection and do a few minutes. How's that sound?' I said, hoping the beggar lurking in my thoughts wasn't too apparent.

'Fine with me,' he replied, flexing his fingers.

As there were only about a hundred people in the audience, the curtains opened to anemic applause. We roared into our two opening numbers, which were greeted by even more anemic applause.

'Ladies and Gentlemen,' I announced, 'For your pianistic delight, I give you Brian —'

I'd called him Rachmaninoff for so long I'd forgotten his last name.

Brian approached the microphone and recited the list of tunes he was going to play to a puzzled audience. Returning to the piano, he started on what he must have thought of as his solo concert debut at the Carnegie Hall. It went on and on and on and on. His performance achieved two major things: It thinned the audience by about 50% and gave us the break we needed.

The Wheel Barrow

An exceptional example of how professional, resourceful and reliable most musicians can be is when the group played a date at a hall at the side of a big pub in Eltham, South East London. The night was sure to be a good one as it was the annual get-together of the South London Fair Ground Association. Though not singers or musicians, those wonderful people were still, in a sense, entertainers — and very much part of show business.

The weather was bad. Damp and drizzle had been present all morning and as the afternoon wore on, a mist, or light fog, began to set in. Like the other guys in the group, with the weather closing in and darkness approaching, I left early. Even so, getting to the pub around 3.30 p.m. the fog was starting to thicken. By 6.00 p.m. a 'pea-souper' had well and truly arrived. At times, with my arm extended in front of me, I couldn't see my hand.

The only person yet to show was the drummer Ray Cooper. After Doug Wright had left, Andy Wight came in to do a few dances and concerts but being busy with his regular schedule his appearances were more of a temporary nature. We were lucky to secure the services of Ray Cooper, a very good and experienced musician. Being the regular drummer with Joe Loss for many years he'd been every where and done everything. The highlight of his time with us, apart from his regular drumming, was his magnificent drum solos. I've said before how the crowds react to drum solos, well, with Ray, they used to go crazy. His sense of the dramatic and the dynamics within his solos had to be heard to be truly appreciated. (That's enough about you, Cooper, back to the fog!) There was no reply when we called his house so our fears were starting to mount. Ray lived in Bexley Heath, a suburb of London and about three miles from where we were working but even that distance, with the severity of the fog, might have well have been three hundred miles.

Standing outside the entrance to the Pub and looking all about me for some sign of Ray, I suddenly became aware of a dim light waving in the gloom. Slowly, through the swirling fog, there emerged a figure

Ray Cooper. Drums, percussion and wheelbarrow.

shrouded in scarves and warm clothing, a cap placed low on his head and, tied to a pole, swung a storm lantern. The pole was secured to a wheel barrow piled high with his drums. Ray staggered to a stop, sweat dripping from his brow, and collapsed on a seat by the entrance. 'I couldn't drive and I couldn't let you down and here I am!' Ray puffed. 'Ave I got a few moments to rest up before I set up?'

The story of Ray's determination to get to this gig had now reached the fairground people who, if anybody would appreciate his efforts, they would. Ray was treated like a king. His drums disappeared inside the hall to magically appear on stage. He was hustled to the bar and plied with hot toddies to get his circulation back and after a short while he was his old self again. The night *was a* good one, finishing about 2 .00 a.m. With the fog slowly clearing, I think I got home about 10.00 the next morning.

It was all part of the glamour of Show Biz.

Both Doug Wright and Les Reed had left the band, and after Rachmaninoff vacated the piano chair for a career at (one hoped for his sake) a higher level, we were pleased to work with Kenny Salmon, another fine musician whose talents did not escape the eagle eye, and ear, of John Barry. As Les was working hard to be a successful songwriter and arranger, he had neither the time nor the inclination to help John Barry with his musical questions, demos or appearances. Presented with the bare minimum of music, Kenny's musical professionalism forced him to fill it out and 'to make something of it.' The 'fillings out' and 'the make something of it' did not escape John's ear holes or his tape recorder. I often wondered how much influence both Les and Kenny had on the success of John's early career.

Concerts

With a busy concert schedule, the Seven got used to driving into towns with no idea where we were playing until we saw the advertising posters. Then, having found the theater or movie house, came the mad scramble to set up as much gear as you could followed by finding some 'digs,' grabbing a meal and getting back to the venue to change and get on stage for the opening. The group's rhythm section was delegated to accompany the whole show — for very little extra recompense, as I remember. Nothing changes!

On the stage of a dilapidated theatre in the North of England, I was sitting at the piano rehearsing with the Lana Sisters (my first encounter with Dusty Springfield) when I started to notice specks of dust on the piano keyboard. Soon there was dirt on the music and on my hands. I looked up to see where the dust was coming from and saw nothing unusual. Returning my attention to the girls and the piano the rehearsal continued. Suddenly there was a grinding sound, a screaming of tortured metal followed by a virtual avalanche of dust and dirt. The two-ton safety curtain had broken free from its locked position and was hurtling down toward my head. With a shriek, both from me and the curtain, the massive object juddered to a halt literally three feet from my head.

I sat transfixed, frozen with fear, staring at the bottom of the curtain.

The stage came alive with stagehands, onlookers, musicians, acts, all trying to do something, but there was nothing to do — except abandon the show.

It was on the same tour when my car, a Rover Sixteen, and my doubtful driving skills gave me another moment of terror. Most of the driving home was done late at night when the roads were almost deserted. The clear roads gave me a sense of freedom that nearly proved fatal. Speeding along a road somewhere in England, I crested a small rise and the car left the road. In front of me was a large truck stopped across the road. Landing with a bone-shaking thud, the car steered itself through a stand of trees, across a grassy bank, over a ditch and back out on to the road where I once again took shaky command.

There were other times that my life and the lives of others were in jeopardy. Once, during a Scottish tour, we were driving along a dark and lonely road when the rear car went missing in my rearview mirror. Members of the Seven wanted to go ahead but I decided to turn back and found the other car on its side in a marsh. The promoter, who already had a broken leg, now had a broken arm. He broke his leg by jumping over a four-foot wall for a pee. Unfortunately, the ground on the other side of the wall was fifteen feet down! Looking for a doctor or any kind of help, we came upon a dark house — miles from any neighbor. Knocking on the door we witnessed a light (probably a candle) moving from room to room and down the stairs to the hallway. An elderly lady, all alone in the house, allowed just one of us to go in and call the police. The rest of us had to wait outside in the cold and windy Scottish night.

The promoter retired from the tour and we never saw him again.

Playing in a small theater in Pontifract, the crew had made the stage more presentable by covering the two 3' by 4' gaps at each side with rubber matting. The King Brothers, a musical trio (Dennis King, the pianist, is now a respected composer) were one of the acts. Dennis walked to the side stage to take his bows — and promptly disappeared from sight. He scraped his side and face quite badly but this didn't distract from the humour of the situation. It's a cruel world.

It was at this theater that we found the dressing rooms to be very much wanting. Not only were they small, there were only two for the whole show. To top off this misery, the sinks had no drainage plumbing attached, so within a few minutes the floors were running with soapy water.

The Seven secured a ten-week season in Blackpool at the ABC Theater with Adam Faith as the star. We used to do Monday through Saturday at the ABC and drive round Great Britain doing concerts; only one Sunday in the ten weeks did we have free. As a treat for my long-suffering bride Judy, we went into town and finished up in the bar at the Blackpool Tower Ballroom. Relaxing with a drink and feeling good about the whole day together, I was accosted by Don Lang of 'Frantic Five' fame. His guitar player had had an accident on his way to the Tower and would not make the concert Don was appearing in. Please, please, would I do the act with him?

Much against my will, and once again leaving my Judy at the side of the stage, I borrowed a guitar and an amp from somewhere and went on stage in an ill-fitting jacket and not too sure of the songs Don was going to do. But, with that glassy smile to the fore, everything, apart from that complete day together, worked out fine.

When a show was put together, musical backing had to be provided for most of the acts, as well as the star. For the show at Blackpool's ABC Theatre, the producers had no trouble. The rhythm section of the Seven was requisitioned to accompany everybody, including Adam, as well as doing the 'standing-up-leaping-about' bit of the Seven's own act. Being on stage all this time was tiring and demanding: the guys needed some distraction. After we finished the first half, which was the Seven's act, we weren't needed till Adam went on to close the show. The comedian Don Arrol did a spot before Adam. This gave us some forty minutes to fill — Don's act plus the interval. The Snooker bug had hit every one of us and, to satisfy this need, we all rushed off to a Snooker Club a few miles out of town. There we would play until just a few minutes before we were due on stage, then drive like crazy back to the theatre, rush on stage just in time to play the opening instrumental number before Adam was introduced. (If members of the audience wondered why the band was out of breath for the first part of Adam's act—that was the reason.)

Adam had his share of traumatic moments, too. The Seven played the first number as an instrumental, like an opening medley, then a voice on the intercom would announce: 'And now, Ladies and Gentlemen, the star of our show — Adam Faith!' On this cue, the trusty stage hands hauled as smoothly as possible on ropes that pulled apart the two parts of the rostrum on which the Seven was set up. The rostrum now became rostra and formed an inverted 'V' that pointed to the back of the stage. Adam would make his grand entrance from the back of the stage through this 'V.' Either the stage hands pulled too fast or stopped too quickly or the wheels found a bump in the stage or a cable got stuck, because many nights it was almost impossible to play and maintain one's balance. I used to play standing up, balancing on one foot with my other foot on a volume/tone pedal. Some nights I had to leap from my rostrum on to the stage and then clamber back on, whilst playing the whole time. The experience was quite daunting and led to some forceful recriminations after the show. Adam, I must say, always put on a great show and the audience loved him.

The M1 from the North Circular to the North of England was completed during my 'touring days' and the Blue Boar Cafeteria became quite a meeting place for groups and the few remaining big bands like Bob Miller and his Miller Men, the Squadronaires, Nat Temple and a few others. Benzedrine was one of the more unsophisticated 'drugs' in use during that period. I won't say which group it was, but whichever musician went to get the tray of teas for the rest of the guys would break up and put half a stick of Benzedrine in one of the cups. So, somewhere down the M1, the recipient of the 'fixed' cuppa would be jumping about in the van and doing all sorts of strange things. Sometimes, as chance would have it, the luckless fellow would be the driver!

There was a group called the Mudlarks who decided to go with the fashion of the Pop stars and bought a large blue American car. They drove it out of the dealership and up the M1 to do some concerts. Halfway up the motorway the engine started making strange rattling sounds, but the driver managed to get the car to the Blue Boar Service Station. A mechanic diagnosed that the engine had never had any oil. The engine was wrecked. He told them to park it at the back of the station and the dealer would take care of it. The building and groundwork were not finished at the station and a retaining wall had not been built. Backing the car to park, the back wheels went over the concrete pavement. The car dropped, bending the body and wrecking the transmission. Within a matter of an hour a brand new, very expensive American car was completely written off.

A big recording star of the period was Marty Wilde. He was famous within the industry for doing the most takes of one song in different studios. (I heard it was 75 takes in three studios — but you know what rumours are like.) I was doing a BBC broadcast — *Saturday Club*, I think — when his manager, Larry Parnes, came rushing in with the news he had got Marty a spot in a prestigious concert at the Regal, Edmonton, a movie theater that held about six thousand people. Would I accompany Marty as I was on the record and had just done the broadcast with him so knowing the song?

'Yes!' I said.

Off we went in a hired limousine to Edmonton where we were whisked onto the stage. We were standing in front of a curtain behind which was the Basil Kirchin Band. A comedian began to announce Marty when suddenly a whole lot of shouting and swearing came from backstage. The noise grew and then just stopped. Marty's name was greeted by screams from the audience and all the curtains were pulled back. Playing the first few bars of solo guitar intro, I turned my head and discovered there was no band! They had stormed off in protest at being shouted at by Marty's manager, leaving me the sole provider of music. Marty turned to me with panic in his eyes and, in a gap in the lyrics, shouted, 'Turn it up!' With the screaming of the audience he couldn't hear my amplifier so I turned my amp up to number 11. Our star still couldn't hear too well!

Now came the *really* funny part. As in most theatres, the Regal's stage sloped toward the audience. The vibrations of my amp caused it to lose traction on the stage and I was appalled to see my amp sliding past me toward the edge of the stage — it seemed to have a life of its own! Still playing, I chased it down the stage and managed to stop the amp's forward movement. My musical and physical heroics still didn't stop Marty from thinking it was entirely my fault; he glowered at me through the remainder of the song.

So ended one of the worst moments of my life.

Talking of Rock stars, I must mention a certain Vince Eager. He was a nice fellow who had some luck on the Pop scene and was also managed by Larry Parnes. We were playing another vast cinema in the north of London and rehearsed in the afternoon with all the working lights on. Vince, like all true pros, used all the stage — even on rehearsals. The night arrived and to the roar of the crowd, Vince bounded on stage, sang two words of his opening song and disappeared from view. We continued to play and, along with banging and scraping sounds on the P.A., came a breathless rendition of the rest of the song. As we entered the last chorus of Vince's opening number, two hands appeared over the front of the stage, followed by a disheveled and bleeding songster. Without telling anybody in the show, the stage crew had lowered the floor of the orchestra pit that had been elevated for the rehearsal. Vince, rushing on stage and blinded by the spotlights, couldn't see that the floor had been removed. He plunged into the darkness below. To give credit where credit is due, he never missed but a few words of the song.

Yet another Rock Star managed by Larry Parnes was Billy Fury. His first ever stage appearance was at a cinema in Whitehaven, a coastal town in the North West of England, somewhere near Liverpool. He stood at the side of the stage shaking with nerves waiting to be thrust before his public. I stood next to him and tried to say a few words of comfort but he looked pale and drawn and was muttering to himself — come to think of it, the perfect Pop Star image of the early sixties. His name was shouted and on he went. He later told me he didn't know how his legs worked to get him on stage. However, his one song on that night, 'Maybe Tomorrow' was a big success and he went on to be a great Star and a good guy to know. Billy was always fascinated by horses and became quite an authority on the subject, as well as owning several thoroughbreds.

Back to Vince Eager.

I got this call to see if I would go with Vince (and a drummer and bass player) to Oxford University. Thinking it was to do some sort of a concert, I agreed. I went to the pick-up point and found a Rolls Royce. In the automobile were the famous reporter and columnist Nancy Spain and some other passengers. I joined them and off we set. I learned there was a debate taking place that evening in the Oxford University Debating

Society about the negative effect of Rock and Roll music on the general public. We parked some distance from the Debating Hall and, led by student conspirators, made our way to a back entrance. Through the door and up the stairs we crept to a landing outside the spectators' gallery. The only source of electricity for the amps was a single bulb fitting hanging from the ceiling. Lifting the drummer up on our shoulders, he managed to plug a fitting in to the outlet — leaving us in the dark. Turning our amps to what was hoped to be a loud level, we waited for the cue from the debating floor.

Sure enough, there came the cry: 'And what do you think of this?'

Upon hearing the cue, Nancy threw open the double doors and we leapt out onto the gallery pounding our instruments in a raucous version of 'Blue Suede Shoes.' Pandemonium broke out as the sounds of voice, guitars and drum filled the hallowed hall. Never — and I mean never — in the long history of the Debating Hall, had music even been allowed. The members of the debating society were out to get our blood. Hastily, we pulled the cable free and trailing wires and cables fled down the stairs, out the door, across a grassy area and into the Rolls — and off we went.

This incident reminds me of the Groucho Marx line: 'The audience was with me all the way — but I managed to shake them off at the station.'

When arriving at a new town and after finding the hall and unloading, the first thing we did was find digs (if we had to). This particular night we didn't need digs as we were all driving back to London, so off we went for a meal. At that time (the early 1960s), it seemed as though the only available restaurants featured Chinese or Indian cuisine. We settled for Chinese. After entering and taking a large table at the back of the restaurant, Les Reed realized he had left his pocket book in the dressing room. He hurried back to get it after telling us what his order was. Fifteen minutes later he was on his way back at a run. Because he was in a hurry and because it was downhill, Les couldn't stop and came crashing through the restaurant door, colliding with the waiter who had a large round tray laden with our order. The explosion of bodies, fried rice, and Chicken Chow Mein had to be seen to be believed. Everyone in that restaurant was picking food off their clothes and out of their hair. The manager was shrieking Chinese obscenities at the top of his voice and the waiters were going to lynch us all, so we made a hasty retreat.

It wasn't the first time we had played a concert on empty stomachs!

The JB7 was booked to be part of a music extravaganza at the Tower Ballroom in Blackpool, the scene of the Don Lang episode. The hall held several thousand people and it was packed. Many stars were appearing and the publicity was everywhere. We were to do a medley of the group's most successful numbers in an eight-minute spot. The first number started with me playing loud, aggressive six-string chords. On chord number two, the second string broke. My guitar had a tremolo arm with compensating springs in the back. Once any string broke and changed the tension, the springs compensated and all the rest of the strings went dramatically out of tune. The piano took over the intro and I rushed off stage to fit a new string. Try as I may, I could not get the old string out of the bridge fitting until the stage manager — using an enormous pair of pliers — ripped off the guitar's back plate and extracted the string.

Meanwhile, on stage, we were finishing the first number in a rather ragged fashion. John Barry cried out in desperation: 'A twelve-bar, for Chris'sake!' The panic was caused by all the numbers we had planned to play being big guitar solos, which made up most of the group's library. However, I fixed the string, and, sweating like some wild animal, rushed back on stage to literally play the last chord. The audience crazily applauded the group's performance — which makes one start to wonder about a lot of things!

The south of London boasted a famous dance hall called The Wimbledon Palaise. Any band worth its salt had played there and always received a warm welcome. We were booked to play a dance date and set up on the stage with the drums on a high rostrum at the back. A special arrangement of 'When the Saints Go Marching In' featured Doug Wright soloing on drums. For some reason or other, the public always applauded drum solos. This knowledge came in useful when the Seven was starting to die a bit on stage. The announcement would be made: 'And now — Doug Wright on the drums!' And the audience would magically spring to life. They crowded round with expectant looks on their faces, their bodies moving as one to the rhythm. The drum solo also gave the rest of the band the time to get off stage and have a smoke.

In preparing for the big moment, Doug had this habit of playing drums with one hand and adjusting his cymbals and stool with the other. On this particular night I think he over-adjusted. He usually played the last couple of bars before the solo whilst the rest of us raised our hands toward the drums. What we saw was a desperate Doug trying to retain his balance by holding onto anything that seemed rooted to the rostrum. Of course, nothing was! He had adjusted his drum stool so that the back leg had slipped over the back of the rostrum. It wasn't one of his better solos, but it certainly was one of his most spectacular. It's amazing how long the human form can suspend itself in space and how many movements it can make before gravity takes over. Doug disappeared in a tangle of tom-toms, snare drums, cymbals, stands and music behind the stage. It took a short while before we rushed to his aid. After all, we'd been denied our smoke, and we had to stop laughing first!

Doug left the group in 1962 and joined The Ted Taylor Quartet, playing and singing in Isos Club in the West End of London. Not the sort of job I would have liked but he seemed happy enough. Later, he started doing sessions and our paths crossed quite often. We even wrote songs together, not one of which did much good. But it was an interesting period.

Back to Blackpool and a gruesome tale. We were rehearsing in the ABC theatre one Saturday morning when the lights went dim and the amplifiers died for a couple of seconds. We thought it was just a power failure and carried on rehearsing. A little while later we noticed a strange smell, like roasting pork, permeating the stage. Again the lights dimmed and the amps died, but this time with much greater effect. Once more this strange smell invaded the stage. Several of us got up to investigate. Maybe a plug was faulty or a lamp colour was touching a bulb. We looked for the electrician on duty but could not find him. Nothing was found and we played through a couple more numbers until we were stopped in our tracks by a series of chilling screams. A cleaning lady had found the head electrician dead. He had electrocuted himself — twice. The first time he hadn't connected enough memories (outlets) to himself; he had succeeded on his second try by connecting more power to his body and by standing in a bucket of water.

We later discovered that this poor man had been caught short and was taking a leak against a tree whilst out for a walk. A busybody policeman had seen him and booked him for indecently exposing himself in a public place. Being a highly respected figure in the community, the shame was too much for him to bear and he took his life before the trial date. I've often wondered how that policeman managed to sleep at night.

An important date in the musical calendar was the New Musical Express Poll Winners' Concert, held at the Wembley Stadium. Everybody who was anybody in the Pop World gathered at these extravaganzas. Drinking a cup of tea at the same table as The Rolling Stones, some of the Shadows, Marty Wilde, and many other luminaries would lead to the swapping of many 'on the road' stories, some of which cannot be retold on these pages. The crowds were enormous, the list of artists was as long as my arm and the sound was dreadful. There was nothing 'high tech' about this presentation. The stage was a scaffolding structure with large black drapes at the back. Access was made from a runway-type structure at the back of the stage along which performers would run up and onto the stage after hearing their name booming around the auditorium. Bands, like Bob Miller and the Miller Men, would be booked to accompany a whole slew of artists, so not only did they have to rehearse with singers and their conductors for lengthy periods, they were also trapped on stage even when not playing. Musicians

Adam Faith and The Seven at the New Musical Express Poll Winners' Concert, 1965

being who they are, always found a way to slip off stage for a smoke (everybody smoked then), much to the consternation of the various conductors. With perhaps a minute before an artist needed accompanying, the luckless musical director would look at a sea of vacant chairs. But — again — musicians being who they are, there would always be a full complement for the down beat.

All the groups had to make do with other musicians' amplifiers and equipment. Drummers would race on clutching their favorite cymbals. With no opportunity to 'sound check,' you just went at it once you had plugged your instrument in, hoping the guy before you had left the volume roughly where you wanted it. Those concerts were a lot of fun; fans and performers alike loved the atmosphere. For some unknown reason I always finished up with an attack of influenza following any appearance at Wembley Stadium. Maybe it was coincidence, but I did get a bit paranoid about taking work there.

The John Barry Seven was riding high on the wave of popularity generated by records in the charts, television, broadcasts and concerts. Bookings were flowing in. One booking in particular was a highlight of all our careers; it came in 1960. We received a gold-embossed invitation from Buckingham Palace to perform at the Royal Variety Performance, or 'Command Performance' as it was affectionately known. We were to appear with Adam Faith at the Victoria Palace along with a host of other stars, both British and International. In fact, there were so many acts that we were forced to use the rooms above a pub across the street from the theatre. Walking across the street carrying our instruments, and in uniform and make up, elicited some strange looks from passersby. Backstage was the usual organized chaos: juggling acts mixing with be-plumed dancing girls, stage hands moving flats with skill and ease through all the props and ropes and theatrical paraphernalia, the stage manager making sure the next act was ready

It was like any other show on the surface but there was this aura of excitement that only a Royal Command Performance can have.

I've been lucky enough to have performed at two such galas. The second was with the Joe Loss Orchestra. I don't think Joe had a hit record or any other fleeting qualification. He was there because of the pleasure and quality of music he had delivered to millions of viewers, listeners and dancers over the years. Joe was a perfectionist and, because of this, he had worked himself up into a bit of a lather over this performance. We had rehearsed the numbers we were going to do many times and the singers (Rose Brennan, Larry Gretton and Ross McManus — Elvis Costello's dad) had sung their songs till they were blue in the face. I was brought in as second guitar to Laurie Steel, Joe's regular guitarist. Two guitars in a band, especially a dance band, was a luxury even on this very special occasion. Laurie, or the 'Electric Imp,' as he was affectionately nicknamed, was a fine guitarist with an individual style. He was also very easy to work with. I had recorded and worked with the Joe's band many times and it was a good feeling to be included on this day. All the musicians who have worked with Joe respect him for the gentleman that he is. After every gig, included with my cheque, was a handwritten thank you note. (There aren't many like Joe about.)

Everything was going perfectly for the show. The band was set up on a three-tiered rostrum. Saxes at the front, then next up were the brass, and on the top was the rhythm section — two guitars, Alan Weighell on bass guitar and drums. The amps were plugged into an ancient-looking socket board supplied by the theatre. That little board was the reason for Joe's big day to start to fall apart. Everything was fine until Rose came on to sing 'The Shrimp Boats Are Coming.' On the first beat of the bar, when the bass and bass drum were at their loudest, the electrics decided to play up. So it was splutter, 2, 3, crackle, 2, 3, pop, 2, 3. Joe started to lose it! His eyes started to bulge and his leaps into the air became Olympian in height. As I said, Joe was in awe of the occasion and didn't want to appear lacking in composure in front of the Queen of England, so all the expressions were directed with his back to the Royals and his face to the band. Joe's gyrations didn't make it easy to keep a straight face, so the wind instrument players found it more and more difficult to play — and this only added to the chaotic situation. Larry Gretton was on the floor at the side of the stage in convulsions.

By this time the electricians had realized what the problem was. But — because the whole set was center stage with about six feet clear each side and no room at the back — no ready access was available to the strip of electrical sockets. The electricians, calling on their vast reserves of technical knowledge, began to throw stage weights and anything else that came to hand at the offending electrical socket strip. This didn't help too much. Coupled with the extra thumps and banging, we lost all power for at least five whole beats, which further aggravated Joe's near-apoplectic condition. By this time, Rose had started to see the funny side of the situation, along with a good part of the audience. She kept gamely on to the end of the song, taking her bows to tumultuous applause.

As we exited the stage, the incident of the Electrical Sockets gently slid into the entertainment history books.

John Barry figured quite prominently in my working life from 1960 onwards. Several times my loyalty was put to the test, but I hung in there till enough was enough and I put in my resignation with six months' notice. Long enough, you might say, but just a week before I was to leave in 1963, JB had still come to terms with the fact I was leaving. Even on the last night — a dance gig the beach resort of Torquay — he got mad because I wouldn't do the next week's schedule. There was nothing I could do. My session schedule was very busy and I wasn't going to start putting deputies in a scene I had worked hard to cultivate. Had I known that JB had blown a solo contract for me with EMI, I would have left a long time before — and with no notice!

Television shows with a large orchestra have become a thing of the past. Isolated shows can be picked out, but the norm today is a small band with maybe the theme pre-recorded. I was certainly lucky to be on the scene in the days of the large television orchestra. Either the broadcasters had a lot of money or the musicians were working cheap but whatever the reason, a lot of musicians were working, the overall standard of musicianship was higher and musical pleasure was being given to millions. On a television series of thirteen weeks there was a temporary kind of permanency, if that makes any sense. Two days' work a week for the next thirteen weeks seemed like a very long time to the session musician. On the day before the show's broadcast or taping, the orchestra was usually called in to rehearse the music for the show and record any titles that were necessary for the production. If a title was pre-recorded and used for rehearsal, then extra money was paid to the musicians. Those little extras like overtime and doubling helped make the pay check more acceptable.

Many artists have an ego that could be sympathized with and, in a strange sort of way, understood. Sacha Distel had an ego that could be understood but not sympathized with. A demonstration of this took place at London's Talk of the Town when he took part in an *International Cabaret* television show. Sacha was a renowned jazz guitarist and a good romantic-type singer who had a hit record in 1970 with 'Raindrops Keep Falling on My Head.' His name was linked to many exotic and famous ladies; musically, he worked successfully with such luminaries as Oscar Peterson and Stan Getz.

Unfortunately for both of us, he also worked with me.

He rehearsed 'Raindrops,' which went well, and another number of which the title escapes me. This other number had an intro where Sacha played the lead on his guitar and I played a harmony line, not an overly complicated few measures but hard enough to have to concentrate. To make matters a little more difficult, Sacha decided to play the intro as he walked on stage. The multi-actions of playing, walking, smiling and bowing to the imagined audiences' applause didn't lend themselves to an accurate performance.

Very quickly, our two musical lines separated and Sacha turned and glared at me. Looking up, I glared back. Sitting on a chair with the part in front of me, my money was on my rendition for accuracy. The number was started again and the same thing happened. He walked over to Alyn Aynsworth the musical director and said, 'Why can't the guitarist get it right?'

Alyn looked at me and asked if I was having trouble with the part. I assured him as firmly as I could that I had no problems with the part as it was written, it was just a matter of Sacha and I getting together — which implied, I hope successfully, that Mr Distel wasn't doing his bit right.

Sacha said nothing and walked quickly away to try the intro and the whole piece again. He got it wrong again. This time he continued on to center stage and sung the number but not before he turned and glared at me and shook his head at Alyn. Alyn was now closely following the written parts on the score in front of him and as soon as the intro finished, looked up at me, smiled and raised his shoulders as if to say, 'What can you do?'

Even on the show, with the cameras running, Sacha got his part wrong and such was his character he took time to turn and glare at me. If he'd just said 'I'm sorry,' everybody would have been happy — and he would have probably played his line correctly!

I have to recount a moment on a Perry Botkin Jr. session that has gone in to recording session folklore. (Perry Botkin, Senior, was, of course, the famous film and orchestral composer.) Botkin Jr. had been commissioned by Readers Digest Records to record an album of his father's music. One of the titles featured the banjo, and the luckless player was Clive Hicks. Most guitar players played banjo as a double, but except for a few musicians like Billy Bell, Judd Proctor and Ernie Shear, it was not an instrument we were overly familiar with and required considerable more concentration to play. Clive hadn't seen his banjo for some time and on the day of the session, extracted it from its dusty case and proceeded to tune it.

On the second or third number into the session, Clive picked his banjo up and prepared to play his part. He had to tune it once again, which was unusual. After several measures into the tune the banjo needed tuning again. Botkin Jr. stopped the orchestra for Clive to retune. Again we started and again we had to stop for Clive to retune. Botkin Jr. was getting impatient and starting to ask questions. Suddenly, the tail piece, which had slowly been working itself loose, separated itself from the banjo's body with a loud bang.

Botkin Jr. cried out from the podium: 'The goddamn thing's in ruins. What are we gonna' do?'

To repair the tail piece meant the back had to come off the banjo, a job that would take a few minutes. Botkin Jr. was now starting to get upset. Glaring down from the podium, he ordered Clive to fix his banjo. Clive laid the banjo on his lap, undid the large screw holding the back on, replaced and tightened up the screw holding the tail piece and put the back on. All this with Botkin Jr. repeating (in a very annoyed and anxious voice): 'Is it ready? 'Can we start?'

'I just have to tune it again,' stated a flustered Clive as he turned the banjo back up from his lap.

We were then confronted with the sight of Clive with the banjo stuck right up under his chin. 'Oh, God!' Clive moaned as he realized what had happened. He had caught his shirt and sweater in the back of the banjo when he's tightened the back. Lifting the banjo from his lap he was forced to tune the instrument in its new position — just under his chin.

Botkin Jr. was in no mood to wait whilst Clive undressed to release the banjo from its ridiculous position so, following the tune up, we launched into the number. It was not easy for any of us to play our parts with a straight face as we sat next to Clive with his banjo perched under his chin, his face and sweater straining with the effort. Botkin Jr. didn't appreciate the humour at all and appeared to read the situation as some disrespectful British plot we had all hatched against a visiting American.

I shall never understand why some people take life so seriously.

Burt Bacharach was always a seeker of perfection in the studio. That part of him had everything to do with his success. His songs were perfect, at least the ones the public got to hear, and his work in the studio consisted of one relentless search for the ultimate recording. I've not met anyone who has worked with Burt say a derogatory word about him. My very close encounter of the double-stopping kind came when the instrumental version of 'Trains and Boats and Planes' was recorded. Pye Recording Studios at Marble Arch was one of Burt's favourites. Setting up in Studio 1, I had no idea that one of the titles was going to be his 1965 single release and go straight into the UK charts at #4.

Most of the guitar part had been written in double stopping, or two notes played together. The physically demanding aspect of the part was the number of glissandos. Sliding up and down the fret board playing two notes caused a lot of friction. Even my hardened fingers were starting to feel the pace after a few rehearsals and a couple of takes. I got some respite when we went into the box to listen to playback but, after a few short minutes, it was back to the grind, literally. On some takes, even when we were close to the end, Burt would wave us to a halt because something like the tambourine wasn't just quite right. I started to glare at my fellow musicians when the smallest mistake caused yet another retake. With a full week's work stretching ahead of me, I didn't want to ruin my left hand for one title. The tips of my left hand fingers were now very sore. After listening to what I hoped to be the final take, Burt sat still for a minute and the asked for another take.

'Burt,' I said, from the back of the control room. 'Physically, this has to be about the last take. My fingers won't make another one after this.'

I have to tell you that my condition had to be critical for me to say what I did. Burt looked at me and I knew that was probably the last time he'd use me on a date. Well, I thought to myself, thank God for all the other musical directors I worked with. One last take did it, and I breathed a sigh of relief.

Whether it was by coincidence or choice I never worked with Burt again, but I was walking into the entrance doorway at PYE Studio a few years later where Burt was just reaching the top of the stairs that lead down to the studios. Seeing me he said. 'Hi, Vic. How're you doing? Where have you been?'

Maybe it was just coincidence I didn't work for him again!

John Cameron is a talented arranger and composer and, on this occasion, musical director. *The Spike Milligan Show* featured Bobby Gentry singing her 1967 hit, 'Ode to Billy Joe.' No matter how famous someone was, everyone had to rehearse with the band, so Miss Gentry approached John Cameron with her music. The parts were handed out and we were all ready to play.

John was a very educated, clever and intelligent man but, like so many of that genre, he had a peculiar quirk. Naturally nervous working with the 'big American star,' John sought sanctuary in his quirk. He wiped his nose with the side of his hand.

Miss Gentry stared with a surprised — nay, shocked — expression on her face and moved back a step. The rehearsal started and stopped a couple of times to clarify some points and each time John did his quirk. Each time Miss Gentry moved back a step, it was almost like a knee-jerk response. I know John had been told about his habit but in times of stress the human body does some strange things. Tell me about it!

Bobby Gentry was great, by the way.

On this show, Spike Milligan, a noted comedian and raconteur, had a complicated routine that only Spike could have dreamed up. As far as I can remember, Spike was to lose his balance on a high rostrum and in a series of rehearsed staggers and stumbles make his way from this rostrum across the set in front of the band onto a rickety table and fall into a large trash can. I can't believe that I can remember that, but that is what I see in my mind's eye. Another ingredient in this already-impossible scenario was the drummer Tony Carr. Tony was Maltese, an all-round percussionist, an expert on Latin American instruments and a very good drummer with a Mediterranean temperament.

On this show Tony played drums, in a style that can be loosely referred to as 'Circus Drums.'

The undeniable experts in the UK of this style of drumming are John Dean and Alf Bigden and, of course, the now-departed Kenny Claire. These talented men can follow any circus act with its tumbles, tricks and acrobatic maneuvers with amazing accuracy yet still keep perfect time. I never ceased to be amazed at their ability. This technique, I hasten to add, does not detract from their ability to excel in all other types of drumming. Of course, to do anything like that correctly the musician has to concentrate on the act, follow the conductor and read the music all at the same time. Tony failed to include one of these elements in that day's performance.

When Spike Milligan had gone through this convoluted and hazardous routine, which he made very clear he didn't want to do more than once, he would end up in the aforementioned large trash can. This triumphant end was to be accompanied by the loudest drumming that Tony could muster which would automatically cut off the band. Due to the lack of rehearsal, Tony completely missed the cue indicated on the drum music for the big finish. Once the dustbin containing Spike had rattled and rolled to a halt, a silence enveloped the studio broken by John Cameron shrieking at the top of his voice: 'Tony! Where were you?'

Tony, up till then paralyzed with professional shock, let forth with a stream of Maltese epithets and kicked his whole drum kit off the stand. The resulting noise brought a smile to Spike's face as it peeked from the dustbin.

'Just the sound I wanted — but a bit late,' he said.

Apart from brief visits to Ireland and Germany, my working was strictly confined to the shores of Great Britain. Not at all a bad thing, but I would have liked to have been more 'international.' I suppose it depends a lot on who you get to work for. Guitarist Clive Hicks got the gig with Charles Aznavour and spent some time touring Europe. Jim Sullivan worked with Tom Jones and got to go to the United States. I was offered the job at Elstree studios when the guitar chair became open but a serious illness in the family took precedence. Big Jim was hired for the job which then led to him doing some great work on the Tom Jones television show. He even became a mini-star with his own spot on the show.

Allan Jones was famous for singing the 'Donkey Serenade.' He was famous for his other work, but that song was forever connected with him, and vice versa. His son was Jack Jones and he is the one that had great success singing his 1963 hit, 'Wives and Lovers.' Working on a television show with him, we were all aware that he seemed to be preoccupied and somewhat aloof in his attitude. Not that we cared how he was, but it's always better to work with someone who is pleasant. We were aware, as the rehearsals ran their course, of this young actress hanging around the studio. Wherever Jack Jones was, she was. It became embarrassing to witness the obsessive nature of her attention. Jones was obviously embarrassed as well.

About that time I'd got this annoying habit, even to me, of mimicking the warble ring of a telephone and would find myself doing it at inappropriate moments. One of these moments was during this television show's rehearsals.

'Someone get that phone,' Jones said into the boom microphone hanging over his head.

What is it that makes people do stupid things? I made the phone sound again for a couple of 'rings.' I have to add that I was on acoustic guitar so my performance as a telephone was being picked up by the microphone in front of me and broadcast throughout the studio.

With a face that resembled a thundercloud, Jack Jones shouted: 'Will someone stop that damn phone from ringing?'

A voice in my headset quietly intoned, 'Vic. Knock it off.' It was a diplomatic warning from the sound engineer that the 'Star' was getting out of control and didn't want any more distractions. The girlfriend had disappeared, so maybe I did Mr Jones a favour.

Studios

London was the centre of the Pop World in the 1950s and 1960s with coffee bars and clubs giving opportunities to the up-and-coming stars of tomorrow. In the West End of London, in Denmark Street — affectionately known as 'Tin Pan Alley' — could be found the music publishing houses of Great Britain. Names like Francis Day and Hunter, Southern Music and Mills Music were printed above large shop-type windows, or painted on swinging metal signs.

Southern Music had adapted a small basement room into a recording studio, supposedly to do demos of the songwriters they had signed up. I thought the 2Is Coffee Bar was bad enough but, *Southern Music Studio*! I used to shudder every time I went to work there. To get to the studio I had to carry my guitars and amplifier down a narrow flight of steps, through the store room with row upon row of wooden shelves stacked with sheet music, and into the small studio at the back. (Rumour has it that Elton John started work in the music business as a sheet music packer in that very store room.) The only escape in case of an emergency from this studio was the way you got in — past all that dry paper and tinder dry wood. If there had been a fire, that place would have been an instant inferno. Even so, many hit records came from that converted broom cupboard.

Regent Sounds Studios in Denmark Street also saw a continuous flow of names that would soon be world renowned. It was a good area to work in with plenty of cafes, restaurants and pubs close by, but there was the ever-present problem of parking. Another small studio (and it barely qualified for the name), was Joe Meek's. Situated above a leathergoods shop in a row of terraced buildings in Holloway Road, North London, Joe's studio was a place where experimentation was an every day occurrence. The recording studio itself was the downstairs front room of a two-bedroom flat which occupied the two top floors of the four-story building. The back room had become the control room and together the two rooms were directly over the flat below. As Joe was occupying the three floors above the shop, there were only mild confrontations with the neighbours when the sound level became too much.

Joe's control room was always a complete mess and only he knew where everything was — and what it did. The floor was permanently ankle deep in cables and spools of magnetic tape. Note paper and posters were stuck on nails banged into the wall and the window was dirty enough to act as a privacy screen. The mixing consul was a put-together concoction of BBC and Army surplus parts. The only respectable things in the place were his two tape recorders. These were Joe's musical instruments. He would play with these two machines into the small hours of the night, getting echo effects and flanging and backward sounds that gave his recordings his very own sound.

Joe could also pick talent. Tom Jones recorded a few titles under Joe's guidance long before he was signed up by Gordon Mills to Decca in 1965. John Leyton started his chart-topping career with Top Rank, recording his songs at Joe's place. I suppose the most famous record to come out of that small studio, and one that set Joe up, was 'Telstar,' recorded by the Tornados and a number-one hit in the UK in September of 1962. (The Tornados were the first British group to have a number-one hit in the charts in America.) To make life easier during sessions, Joe had removed the doors separating the two rooms. Starting his tape recorder, he would appear at the door opening and quietly say something like, 'Go on, then,' and stand watching you play throughout the length of the song. Or perhaps he might lean on the old upright piano. Covered in blankets and other material in an effort to isolate the sound, the piano must have been quite a comfortable lean.

Joe was a genius and a man before his time. What he would have done with today's technology boggles my mind! Unfortunately, being a genius had its problems, problems that over took him and led him to take to his own life. That was a sad time for all those who knew and respected him and his work, and it was a great loss to the music industry. I see in the music recording industry catalogs of the late 1990s, effect units with the name JoeMeek emblazoned across them. I suspect that very few purchasers of that equipment know the story of the man who inspired them. Perhaps a fitting tribute and one for which I thank the manufacturers, even though they have purposely joined his two names together.

Decca Studios at 165, Broadhurst Gardens, West Hampstead, was a complicated building. If you were booked at Decca and were not sure which studio you were in (and you were in a hurry), you might have to lug all your gear through corridors, past offices, secretaries and editing rooms to the studio you were in. Studio 1 was the first studio you came to after entering the front doors on Broadhurst Gardens. Its design was reminiscent of a rice-producing hillside in China with the various levels ascending to the large glass window of the control room. I remember recording 'Black is Black' in Studio 1 with Ivor Raymond as the musical director. It was also the starting place for Anthony Newley's 'Strawberry Fair.'

Studio 2 was in the basement and was the home of many hit recording artists — Tom Jones and Engelbert Humperdinck, to name but two. A highlight of working in Decca 2 in the mornings was the crusty cheese rolls served at the tea break. Two ladies, dressed in white overalls, held court behind a small hatch cut in the wall of a long corridor from which they dispensed mugs of tea and the cheese rolls - and the rolls were delightful. Thick wedges of cheddar cheese, thick spread butter and a crisp, crunchy bread roll. These delicacies, chased down by a hot mug of tea, and any musician would have been ready to take on the world! That's if he hadn't already rushed round to the pub on the corner.

Studio 3 was enormous. It was used for recording large orchestras, choirs and even marching bands. The occasional small group Pop session recorded in Studio 3 never felt quite right. For good reason musicians fondly nick named the studio 'The Tram Shed.' To work and to become an accepted musician at all the recording Studios in London made me very proud. The musicians I had the good fortune to work with were of the highest standard. Some international musical directors, Henry Mancini amongst them, have said that the London musicians were indeed the best in the world. In the 1960s studios such as EMI and Decca were world class and were turning out some wonderful recordings.

But smaller studios were also starting to make an impact. The oldest and most respected independent film music recording studio must be CTS. It was certainly the studio where the majority of the James Bond film scores were recorded and all of the early ones when CTS was located in Bayswater. A big studio, it lent itself both physically and acoustically to film work. The control room was large and accommodating and afforded an excellent view of both orchestra and screen. I worked there many times and felt very comfortable. The recording engineer on the first few Bond films was Eric Tomlinson, a very professional and pleasant person to work with. Eric left CTS and moved out to Denham Studios where a lot of the Dimitri Tiomkin film scores were recorded.

The engineer who stamped his personality on both the old CTS and the new CTS at Wembley was, without a doubt, John Richards. Amazingly cooperative and technically knowledgeable, John amassed a formidable list of clients — including me. If I was recording a music track and the budget allowed for a top studio, CTS and John were my number-one combination and choice. I had written the music for a film about Waterford Glass entitled *Conquest of Light*, an eleven-minute film with wall-to-wall music and just four spoken lines, two at the beginning of the film and two at the end. The music was divided into six cues that overlapped each other, dovetailing when put together by the music editor. I rehearsed the first cue, recorded it, and went up to the control room to listen. The projection room was encountering some trouble so John had yet to see the picture and how my music related to it. John had recorded the cue well and I was happy but we had to be sure the music fit the picture. After rehearsing the music to the picture for John's benefit, we recorded it once again. It was that one cue that convinced me what a great talent John had. Having now seen the picture, he had understood what I wanted and had changed the balance so subtly that every nuance had been brought out - and some that I didn't know were there! The music and picture were a perfect blend. The producer, who also directed the film, was ecstatic. So was I.

Like the smell of perfume or the sound of a melody, just picturing the inside of a studio can bring back memories for me. For instance, the conductor and composer of some film music being recorded at CTS was Italian and very demonstrative with his conducting. As a rhythm section player, it always helps if you can see where the beat is: This is what a conductor is for. Some are so affected with their movements that it's like watching a ballet dancer — and this Italian gentleman was no exception. Waving his arms and moving his body about like a palm tree in a hurricane, he became an object of fascination for the three guitarists and the bass player that had been set up line abreast at the side of the studio. There was Clive Hicks, Bryan Daly and myself on guitars and Dave Richmond on bass. So fascinated were we by his gesticulations that we decided to give him marks for his performances. On the plain back pages of music that had already been recorded we wrote big numbers after each music cue. Waiting for the recording to stop, we would then hang these numbers over the back of our music stands, the score looking like the result of an ice-skating competition. I have to mention that a row of large screens separated us from the rest of the orchestra - and the fixer! 'Mr Italian' looked over a few times and seemed to note the numbers. Unable to contain his curiosity any longer, he stepped down from his podium and came across to the four of us.

'Wadd'a ze numbers a'for?' he asked in broken English.

We told him it was for his score.

'My'a scor'a? For'a wadd'a?'

With straight faces we informed him it was for his performance as a conductor.

'Oh, I'a see,' he said, and returned thoughtfully to the podium.

From then on our Italian friend — and I call him this because he was our friend — would look over to see what score we had given him - and actually bow to us when we gave him four '9s.'

As a contrast, a very serious American conductor had written this complicated harpsichord part that the player was having a little difficulty with. The session was in the afternoon and a few of the orchestra had been across to the pub. The combination of some exotic food concoction and a few glasses of red wine had proved a stumbling block to a perfect performance by our unfortunate pianist (whose name I know but won't reveal). He had been forced to jettison a good part of his lunchtime feast into the keyboard of the harpsichord shortly after the start of the session. The conductor was starting to get irate with the pianist's inability to play the part perfectly — as I hasten to add — could have done under ideal conditions.

'I'll just have to come over there and show you how I want that passage played,' the conductor said.

A silent and concerted 'Oh, no!' could be felt coming from the surrounding rhythm section. Making his way through the music stands and instruments, the musical director's steps began to falter as he caught a glimpse of the mess dripping from the keyboard. The smell wasn't too good either. To give the man credit, he did make a quick decision. Turning on his heel he returned to the podium and asked us to turn to the next cue. He then went to the control room, had a word with the fixer, and a very short while later our defeated pianist was escorted from the studio. Both he and the harpsichord were replaced in the break and the sessions continued.

I find myself reliving the whole episode when I smell a cheap red wine.

Coffee, anyone?

The new CTS at Wembley was purpose built and has always contained the most up-to-date equipment available. The main studio at CTS had been painted in depressing shades of dark purple and mauve. It could host up to eighty musicians in comfort and acoustic screens of all sizes were available to separate the various sections. A technical moment of horror played itself out at the new CTS. I had composed the music for a film made for the tourist office of Jersey, one of the Channel Islands off the coast of France. The director wasn't one of the nicest people on this planet and he was a little abrasive to me. I was not his first choice — I don't know who was, but he certainly managed to give me the impression that I wasn't. This director, the film editor and I went through the twenty-minute film spotting the music from which I was supplied with a copy of the detailed timings. Comes the recording session and we are all assembled in CTS Studio 1. We rehearse the first cue and then ran it to the picture. After the first twenty seconds, the music and picture went out of sync.

Impossible, I thought to myself. I treble checked every detail. I know the music fits.

'Vic, come up to the box for a moment,' John Richards said over the intercom, with just a hint of doom in his voice.

Immediately, I arrived in the control room the director pounced on me: 'Didn't you get the timings? Nothing is going to fit! What the hell do you think you're doing?'

I knew I was right, so I had to take a stance. 'I worked from the timings we agreed on and those were the timings I left the editing suite with. I *know* what I'm doing!'

'Well, it doesn't look like it from what I've just seen,' the director said, showing his true character.

'What it looks like to me,' I said, 'is that you gave me television timings at twenty-five frames a second and we're running the film at cinematograph twenty-four frames.'

'Absolute rubbish!' the director shouted. 'I've been in this business too long to make that mistake. Anyway, I had the machine calibrated only the other day, so it's got to be right.'

The argument continued. I was conscious that I had a medium-sized orchestra in the studio. Not only was the clock ticking away, but the musicians were starting to get up from their chairs, move around, and socialize, which was not a good sign. They were all concerned for me in my dilemma, God bless 'em, and wanted the session to continue successfully. However, it was my problem and certainly nothing they could fix. I hadn't noticed, but the editor had quietly left the studio control room to go back to his office and check the machine.

'If the problem is what I think it is, then I can fix it by recalculating the click track. Give me a few moments,' I said. It is a calculation that I have long since forgotten as it is something that can now be instantly worked out on a computer. After a few minutes of concentration I gave John Richards the new click tracks for all the cues and hoped for the best. They all worked fine.

There is a phone attached to the podium at CTS for making private and discreet calls. About an hour after the incident in the control room the phone rang. It was the director.

'The machine was calibrated to 25 frames,' he said. 'I'm sorry for doubting you.'

'Please repeat that over the studio speakers, I can't hear you too well on this phone,' I said and replaced the receiver. There was a short pause, and then the large playback speakers in the studio blurted out his apology.

Keith Grant is an icon of the recording world. Virtually the resident recording engineer at Olympic Studios, Keith saw the transition from a small mews studio in Carton Place, off Baker Street, to the recording studio complex at Barnes, southwest London. Olympic at Carton Place was one of my favorite studios. Always a friendly atmosphere, the staff was helpful and the sounds that came out were good.

The mews where Olympic was situated was typical of the many to be found in London. A cobbled street with garages and small mews cottages, Carton Place was a little sanctuary just a few yards from the bustle of Baker Street and Oxford Street. Best of all, it was possible to park your car there, un-ticketed, all day. At the end of the street was a working men's cafe that sold mugs of tea and a typical English breakfast could be had if you got there early enough. Bacon, eggs, tomatoes and fried bread would be piled on the plate, with a side of toast and butter. Being a big eater, this was a favorite place of Big Jim Sullivan's. Jim holds the record of eating, at one sitting, three breakfasts, similar to the one I've described above. But Jim, as I've mentioned before, does his own thing.

It was lovely and uplifting on a sunny spring morning to walk from the cafe, past the brightly painted mews cottages with their colourful flower boxes and into the studio. The little mews has now gone and been replaced with some shops, residential properties, plastic pubs — and concrete. Keith knew Olympic Sound Studios as if it were part of him. He would breeze into the studio a few minutes after the start of the session, move about placing and adjusting mikes, catching up with the latest gossip and generally making everybody feel welcome and at home. Many is the time he would then climb the stairs to the control room, look out the large window, smile and say, 'OK. Let's take one,' without having heard a sound from anybody. He knew us all and knew our equipment. We all had our volume levels set approximately the same, day in and day out, so Keith was confident there weren't going to be too many surprises. Sometimes that first take was very good, with only just a few refinements needed.

The move by Olympic Studios to Barnes was caused by two events. One, the studio was becoming busier and busier and needed more space, and two (and probably the most compelling event), the whole area was being razed and redeveloped. Another studio in the same area, Audio International, is still going strong. Actually, Audio International was one of the places I managed to put my big foot in it. Many years ago I worked off and on for Wally Stott, a brilliant arranger and orchestrator. I had often wondered why he seemed depressed. Later, of course, this was explained by the inner torment he must have suffered in connection with his sexual identity. I was actually present at the first session he worked on when Wally Stott had become, with the aid of a sharp knife, Angela Morley.

The transition was wonderful. Not only because of the way she looked and dressed but how happy she was. Of course, this took a bit of getting used to. Angela had brought an arrangement to the studio and was waiting with the musicians for the tea break to end. Of all the musicians there, she turned to me and asked where the bathroom was. I directed her and she turned and went down the steps I had indicated. It was then I became aware of the strange looks on my colleagues' faces. I had directed Angela to the *men's room!* Angela reappeared and as she walked past me, smiling, and said, 'A natural mistake, Vic,' then continued on in the correct direction. It took a while for me to live down that story. Stan Roderick, a fine trumpet player who had known Wally/Angela for years would not or could not acknowledge the change and would always call her Wally — even when Angela was dressed in her prettiest outfit.

Whilst on the subject of Stan Roderick, an event comes to mind that happened at the Kingsway Hall. This hall was large and acoustically quite good and used by record companies to record large orchestras. Due to the layout, the control room was tucked away at the back of the stage. Communication was by microphone and TV Camera. One day at a session, guitarist Ike Issacs was sitting next to me and in front of Stan and was quietly minding his own business. Stan could be very aggravating and on this occasion started to bait Ike. When Ike didn't rise to the bait, Stan had to make sure he was going to win the day. Lighting a piece of newspaper then extinguishing it so it smoked, Stan stuffed it under Ike's chair. With smoke rising all around him, Ike at first thought his amplifier had caught on fire, then, discovering the smoking newspaper he looked round and saw Stan's red and laughing face.

Ike lost it. Standing up and glaring at Stan, Ike swung his guitar, which even in the mid-seventies would have been worth a few thousand pounds, over his head and aimed it at Stan. With a whoosh, the guitar cut its way through the smoky air to stop just inches short of Stan's head — held there by the straining guitar cable. Stan had stopped laughing and had started loudly apologizing. In the control room the producer Tony Demato looked helplessly at the TV monitor as the drama unfolded. Flustered and out of breath, Tony appeared from the back of the stage to try and calm things down. Recriminations followed, but in the end, the incident was written off to tension and stress.

Keith Grant used to like a practical joke and who better to practice on than the poor defenseless musicians lined up in front of him on the studio floor. His favorite jokes involved the head sets. If the session was starting to get a bit 'doomy,' or when there was a particularly unpleasant conductor, Keith would step into the breach with his little bag of tricks. Knowizng that the rhythm section wasn't actually playing at the time, suddenly, a completely different piece of music would be in the headsets. Keith would get great joy out of the looks on our faces as we struggled to keep our minds on the job at hand. One of Keith's specialties was playing 'Hitler Tracks' in the headsets. Your ears would be bombarded with segments of Hitler's speeches in German. This would be accompanied by the sound of massed marching boots on gravel, and gunfire, shouting and all sorts of war noises. Looking up into the control room you could see Keith 'tee-heeing' to himself, hiding his face from the producer with a control sheet or tape box. The conductor would not understand the expressions on our faces, but as he was more often than not a miserable specimen and so provoking the sounds — tough luck.

With one particularly obnoxious conductor on the podium, Keith executed his killer joke. Unfortunately, it was on me! The then latest technology was called a 'harmonizer.' This little box could change the pitch of the note going out from the note coming in. The note going in was my acoustic guitar playing a solo, accompanied by a gentle string pad, and the note coming out was being played only in my head set. Keith had the control part on the desk in front of him so could read what I was playing and adjust accordingly. Arriving at my solo, I started to play the line which, let us say, moved up the scale from middle 'C.' Keith was adjusting the pitch so no matter what note I played, it always sounded like middle 'C.'

Now this can be disconcerting. The conductor's headset was from a different feed so he was oblivious to what was going on. The musicians around me could hear both parts — the one I was playing and the one coming from the headsets — and were enjoying the sounds and my expressions. If you didn't know it before, musicians have a sadistic streak in them. I, who had the headset firmly placed on both ears and could hear only my part through the headset, was becoming increasingly bewildered but determined to finish the passage. Can you imagine? No matter what I played, it always sounded the same one note. I'm flattered, in a sort of backhanded way, that Keith chose me to experiment on as some people could have become very upset.

Keith was at the control desk in Olympic when I recorded the music for a short film called *Ireland Ours*, for the Irish Tourist Board. Around the late '60s or early '70s I composed music for many documentaries. This was partly due to the rates imposed by the UK Mechanical Copyright Protection Society for world clearance of music used in film. Those rates made it worthwhile for me to compose music, with the promise of royalties to come, as opposed to the Production Company paying to use unsuitable library music. The orchestra was about ten musicians strong and included a very proficient, all-round woodwind player, Bill Povey. I rehearsed one particular music cue, recorded it and went into the control room to listen.

Halfway through, I said to Keith, 'What's that strange noise?'

To which Keith replied. 'Bill Povey!'

We continued to listen, without another word being spoken.

Taking advantage of everything that took a rise out of the business, Keith had pinned an enormous poster of the Royal Philharmonic Orchestra on the wall of the studio. Nothing out of the usual one might think, except the picture had been reversed at printing. All the musicians in the orchestra appeared left handed. A very strange sight!

Going east along the Bayswater road, you eventually came to Marble Arch. In a small street one block from this busy junction and directly opposite Hyde Park was Phillips Recording Studio. Set in the basement of a well-maintained large Georgian style house, the studio had a slightly clinical air about it. Everything always seemed so neat and tidy - a direct contrast to Joe Meek's establishment. The control room had the latest equipment including, if I remember correctly, one of the first Neve Recording Consuls. Neve, of Cambridge, went on to be a major player in studio mixing desks throughout the world. The studio was run efficiently by Peter Olaf, the recording engineer. Tall, smartly dressed and with dark-rimmed spectacles, I never saw Peter get ruffled even though there was often justification. Although part of the huge Phillips conglomerate, the studio time wasn't always fully taken up with that company's recording artists so, like most of the other studios, they hired the facility out to independent labels or even individuals just wanting to record a couple of songs.

One such instance involved two Frenchmen who had booked Phillips Studio to record three of their songs. One was the singer and the other was the producer. It soon became evident that their studio experience was limited. The arrangements left a lot to be desired and, coupled with language barriers, the session didn't turn out to be one of the best I've been on. Nevertheless, it left the musicians with a very humorous memory. After we had run the number through a couple of times, the singing Frenchman (who was also conducting) stood in the middle of the studio and started shouting to his friend in the box. He was obviously told to talk into a microphone because he came up to one of the mike stands and started talking. Not into the mike, but into the black plastic handle at the other end of the boom. With the singer bent over, gripping the mike stand and still shouting as loud as he could, things were starting to get out of control. The Frenchman in the control room came stomping into the studio and shouted into the face of the singer something in gutter French that sounded a bit like 'Use a microphone!'

With that, he stalked back into the box.

Those of us close enough to the singer to say something tried to explain what he should do, but to no avail. This man continued to shout into the wrong end of the mike stand for the whole session, to such an extent that he couldn't sing, which drove the man in the box to an even higher apoplectic level. I think that date was the end of a friendship and a singing career.

Phillips was also the home of Top Rank Records. A record company set up by a division of Top Rank it had a few hits with singers John Leyton and Craig Douglas and imports such as B. Bumble and the Stingers, Dion, and The Shirelles. Top Rank had a big hit with the Ventures recording of 'Walk Don't Run,' but the record company also had a lot of misses. Dick Rowe, who had been a big wheel at Decca, had been appointed chief A&R man at Top Rank and proceeded to spend one hell of a lot of money. This made lots of work for recording musicians but, after the initial successes, the company lost its impetus and faded.

Dick Rowe made a good Chief A&R man. He would delegate artists to other A&R men to supervise and record, and generally oversaw projects like a mother hen. The trouble for the other A&R men was, that if their artist had a hit, it was Dick Rowe's idea; if the artist's record failed, it was the other A&R man's idea.

Always slightly aloof in the studios, Dick had a surprisingly kind side to him.

Once, during the 1960s, I went down to the South of France for a MIDEM at Cannes. MIDEM is the annual gathering place of the world's recording businesses and it's the place to make those big international deals. Traveling down through France with Judy in the train, we arrived at Cannes Railway Station at some ungodly hour like 5.15 a.m. The journey was horrendous and unless the comfort level has changed dramatically in recent years, it is not a means of transport to be recommended. Hearing that Judy and I were arriving the next morning, Dick offered to meet us at the station and drive us back to where we were all staying in Juan Le Pin. This meant Dick getting up at 4.00 a.m. Meeting us, he was a different person than the man I thought I knew. Cheerful and full of all the MIDEM news, he made the journey to the hotel a quick and pleasant one. The South of France air must have agreed with Dick.

That period was back when the British Government had slapped a cap on how much money you could take out the country (I think it was about 100 pounds, or something totally inadequate). As an average round of drinks in the Martinez Hotel was about 50 pounds, the British publisher's representatives were forever on the phone begging for more money to be wired to them. The Americans, the Italians and French were all hiring expensive cars and dining at the best restaurants and flashing wads of money about while the poor British were confined to back street Cafes and local bars. Still, a good time was had by all.

I worked in Phillips with some very successful artists — Dusty Springfield, the Walker Brothers, Sandie Shaw, Chris Andrews, Twinkle, and many others. Sandi Shaw had a number-one hit in May of 1967 with the Eurovision Song contest-winning song, 'Puppet on a String.' Her musical director, Kenny Woodman, was very much in demand and somewhat in the Arthur Greenslade mould. Thinking back to a BBC producer who wouldn't allow the Fuzz Box on his show, I wonder what he thought of Sandi's 'There's Always Something There to Remind Me' with my fuzz-tone guitar being so prominent. A little zany, with her bare feet and emotional entanglements, Sandi was good to work with and approached her singing in a very professional manner.

Within just a few hundred yards of Phillips Studio was PYE Recording Studios. PYE was a great example of Star Power. I was early for a session there and wandered into the control room of Studio 1 to find the chief sound engineer, Ray Prickett, sitting behind his control desk looking extremely depressed. The desk looked like a war zone.

'What the hell happened here?' I asked.

It turns out that Frank Sinatra was due to record his 'London' album in PYE Studios and to celebrate this event, the entrance, stairway and the main corridor had been painted silver with a couple of fancy blue lines on the walls. Very chic! All stars have their entourages, but with Sinatra, he had a pre-entourage which consisted of a group of gentlemen that went ahead of Frank to check to see if all was well. One was a bull-necked man wearing a fedora; he wanted to know where the elevator was. There was no elevator, he was informed; only stairs.

'Mr Sinatra don' like stairs,' he stated and the whole group turned and departed.

The Sinatra sessions were promptly transferred to the Old CTS In Bayswater, which was a 'walk-in-from-the-street' studio. No elevator or stairs.

Now comes the complicated part. Frankie had to have everything recorded twice at the same time on completely independent equipment — a facility that PYE had but CTS didn't. So, as the contract was with PYE, half of the desk and other equipment in Studio One was ripped out and transported to CTS to comply with the singer's wishes — hence the disconsolate expression on Ray's face. He wasn't looking forward to putting it all back together again. The session I was to take part in had been transferred to Number 2 studio. I would liked to have worked on Sinatra's album. He used great arrangers like Nelson Riddle, whom I admired immensely.

Being a big studio complex, EMI employed staff to move screens and heavy equipment as needed. One of these 'humpers,' as we called them, used to make a point of helping me with my guitars, amplifier and bag. I could manage OK on my own but, as he insisted, I let him get on with it. Gradually I started to notice he was always there when I was. I don't know how he found out, but he was always there. Then he asked me on one occasion where I was going for lunch in between the morning and afternoon sessions — hinting to go with me. Being as vague as I could, I said I was just going round the corner. I couldn't wait to get out the studio and away from him.

The final straw came when this person sat on a chair by the studio doors staring and smiling at me all the time through three sessions. At one time he actually blew a kiss in my direction. I was starting to get worried. As soon as the last session finished he stood up and ran toward me through the band. I was totally embarrassed and told him to get lost.

'No. No. Let me help you!' he said, trying to grab one of my guitars.

I thought for one horrible moment he was going to start all that 'I love you' crap. If he had, I would have died on the spot. Again, I told him where to go in no uncertain terms. He pouted and slunk away.

On the advice of the other musicians and the recording engineer I reported him to the Studio Manager. I was very pleased not to see him again.

At the other end of Studio 2 from where that strange person sat was another large soundproof door. This led into a small corridor at the end of which was another door to the outside which in its turn led to a short cut to the nearest pub. Very often, either at a 'tea break' or if members of the orchestra were not needed for a lengthy period of time, this exit was used in the course of a session for a quick getaway. All was well until one fateful day as some musicians were returned from an unofficial break while the red light was on — a light not seen inside the short, linking corridor. Not a big deal until you know that access was gained through another door in this corridor to EMI's very own and very special 'Echo Chamber.' This was a large room with smooth angular walls containing an assortment of glazed drainage pipes. Sounds were fed through a speaker at one end of this room to be picked up by a microphone and returned to the mixing desk as that special 'EMI Sound.' Certainly, no other studio had such a facility to give a natural echo. Because of the super sensitivity of the equipment, sounds in the corridor were easily picked up by the microphone in the room. Unfortunately, on this one occasion, the sounds picked up were mostly words uncomplimentary to what was going on in the studio. So those cryptic comments amplified and with a halo of echo, completely ruined the take. From that moment on the use of this exit was banned.

It was another case of musicians spoiling a good thing.

EMI Studio 2 was where the Beatles recorded their epoch-making hit records. Their music did change the course of Pop music at a time when change was needed. Of course, no one knew what a worldwide effect the group would have. Working at EMI almost every other day, I met John, Paul, Ringo and George several times. Studio 2 was exclusively theirs when they wanted to record, any session that may have been booked there were moved to Studio 1 or 3. Not always the best studios for the various types of production but, hey, these guys were paying a significant part of the rent.

IBC was a studio in a Regency type row of buildings just up the road from BBC headquarters, quite near Regents Park. A session was taking place while, just a hundred yards away the Chinese Embassy was under siege. Sometime during the 1960s there was an acute political situation where the Chinese Embassy isolated itself from Great Britain. The windows were boarded up, guards patrolled the roof and at the height of the confrontation demonstrators and the public were kept at a discreet distance by the London police. This police activity made movement and parking around IBC and the BBC, which was already difficult, nigh on impossible. The security clampdown must have caused the Chinese to change their radio frequencies because, suddenly, strange Chinese voices started coming out of our amplifiers when we worked at IBC. Just to think, that with a Fender Stratocaster as an antennae and an amplifier as a receiver, I could have started my own revolution. Better still, with a Chinese interpreter sitting in during a session, the whole political incident could have been over in a tea break!

Not far from IBC and the BBC could be found AIR London, a good and busy studio in a prime location at Oxford Circus. Prime, that is, for artists and staff who were either brought in by taxi or used public transport but not so prime for those musicians who had to bring their cars in and drop off instruments and equipment. After finishing a session at Olympic at Barnes and rushing through the lunch hour traffic to Oxford Circus, the thought of dumping gear and finding a parking place in the heart of the West end was not a good one. Still, it had to be done as the session would have to start and you would have to be there. I am pleased to hear that AIR Studios is now called Air Lyndhurst at a parkable location.

During one of the IRA's bombing periods I was in Air London's small studio recording a jingle for Air Adele with music by Gerry Butler. All was going well until Gerry asked the control room if they were ready for a take. No answer. Again Gerry spoke into his microphone and again there was no answer. We all then noticed that the control room was empty; there was not a soul to be seen. Suddenly the studio door burst open and a security guard stuck his head in and asked,

'What the fuck are you lot still doing here? Get out! They're going to blow the bloody building up!'

With that, the door slammed shut and he was gone.

We all grabbed what was important to us: guitars, basses, cymbals etc, and made for the exit. The danger didn't stop Gerry's sense of humor. 'I didn't think the music was that bad,' he quipped as we made our escape. The studio staff had done a runner as soon as they had got the alarm and 'forgot' to tell us. Their respective parentages were put into considerable doubt when we found out what had happened.

With the bomb threats, the road works and the London traffic, the session musicians had to be admired for their tenacity as much as their musicianship. The ability of musicians to get to studios and park was the least consideration of studio owners and planners. In Bond Street, for example, one of the busiest streets and areas in London, there were Levy's Studios, Chappell's and the BBC all within a few hundred yards of each other. Levy's was a small studio on the second floor of this ancient office building in Bond Street. Originally owned and operated by Oriel Records and later bought out by CBS as their London office, the studio was managed by Jacques Levy. At that time Geraldo had offices for his orchestra and agency in the same building. One damp autumn evening I was waiting at the curbside outside the building for a cab when I was confronted by this elderly lady, who I later found out to be Mrs Geraldo. She looked at the guitars and the amplifier clustered around my ankles and asked.

'Are you a Group?'

'No,' I replied. 'I'm just a musician.'

'Pity. I was looking for a Group for one of our Cruise Ships.'

I have to say, that as I surveyed the traffic jam in Bond Street, the offer of a job on a cruise ship seemed very tempting. Momentarily slipping into a reverie of blue waters, warm sunshine and cold beer, I returned to reality to see Mrs Geraldo stepping into one of the very rare empty cabs. I must try that one, I thought, (confusing the enemy) the next time I want a cab.

Levy's studio was lucky to have Mike Ross as its recording engineer. Embassy Records, which made covers of the latest hit records, used Levy's studio and Mike was a great help in easing the burden of getting a lot of sometimes-difficult music recorded in the three-hour session time. There was a period when I worked at Levy's two sessions a week and Lansdowne Studios two sessions a week doing covers for different companies. It made me listen to music programs on the morning drive-in instead of talk programs. I used to get a clue of what I was in for. Mick later moved to CBS in Goodge Street and was (and is) responsible for some outstanding recordings, *Atlantis, the lost Empire* and *Wind in the Willows* being just two film music tracks he recorded.

Jacques Levy was a pedantic type of man whose attention to detail was both amusing and annoying. He was forever diving in and out of the control room moving microphones a fraction of an inch or shifting the angle of a sound screen. A minute later he would be out in the studio again putting everything back as it was. At last he would scurry back to the control room and announce in dramatic tones: 'Take One!'

One day we arrived at Levy's for the Embassy recordings to find new carpet had been fitted where the rhythm section and percussion were usually placed. New music stands had also appeared with shiny ash trays clamped to them. (Everybody smoked in those days so ash trays were a necessity.) From then on, no matter what size the orchestra or how strapped for time we were, Jacques would go back to the control room and announce his celebrated 'Take One' and even as the music was being counted in, he would say in equally stern and commanding voice: 'Gentlemen, please use the ash trays!'

I never listened, but I'm sure that the word 'trays' must have been over the first beat of many an Embassy cover.

(This 'ash tray' story is the favorite of film director, editor and friend, David Capey, who always roars with laughter whenever he thinks of it. David was wonderfully creative, but he was never known for his attention to details such as ash trays.)

Chappells Recording Studio, further down Bond Street, was managed by John Timperly, an equally professional and experienced recording engineer. Always a perfectionist, John could be easily 'wound up' as his concentration on getting the job done correctly wouldn't always allow him to see the funny side of things. John's studious look and dark-rimmed glasses earned him the nickname of the 'Train Spotter.' This refers to a peculiarly British hobby where people from school age to pensioners would stand beside railway tracks or on bridges 'spotting' railway engines. This entailed noting and writing down the engine number and its wheel configuration, i.e. 0-6-0 or 4-6-2, going home and checking the number in a book of English railway locomotives. Looking back, it's hard to see the attraction of such a past-time, but I used to do the same thing with London busses, recording LST and ST or whatever, and the bus number.

We had been at Chappells for many days recording albums for Anita Kerr, of 'The Anita Kerr Singers' fame. The musicians decided to buy John a present. During one lunch break a quick trip to Gamley's Toy Shop in Regent Street they secured a shiny Hornby model railway signal which was ceremoniously placed on top of one of the big speakers in the control room. It was a good hour into the afternoon session when John pressed the talk back button and said, 'You bloody rotten lot!'

Whatever John actually thought, that signal was dusted regularly and stayed on that speaker for as long as I can remember. John left Chappells, presumably with his signal, when he was persuaded to go to Switzerland and be the recording engineer at Anita Kerr's private studio.

Anita Kerr's husband, Alex Grob, had this idea for a series of albums with titles like 'Chairman of the Board' and 'Director of Music.' Anyway, I was Chairman of the Board and recorded twelve titles which were subsequently taken back to Switzerland and locked in a vault. To paraphrase Gerry Butler's quip: 'I didn't know my music was *that* good!'

One bleak winter's day following the recording, Alex and I met by chance outside Chappells on the corner of Bond Street and Maddox Street. He started to explain yet again his concept of the above-mentioned albums and what a good start I had made with the first one. Alex had just flown in from Switzerland so was suitably dressed for the sub-zero weather we were experiencing. I was in the process of dashing for my car with just a light top coat to protect me. When Alex decided to explain something he really explained something just as, when the chill wind decided to blow round that exposed corner, the wind really blew. I was caught between the explaining and the blowing. I never saw Alex again and it took me a good two days to get warm.

One of the worst studios for parking must be Trident Studios, just off Wardour Street. A session booked after 10 a.m. meant an almost impossible task of trying to park. However, once your car had been parked on a meter (if you could find one), or in an off street parking lot (if you could afford it), the actual studio was very pleasant even though access to the studio floor was down Lansdowne Studio-type stairs.

Malcolm Mitchell used Trident to record the music for his convention shows. Events such as introducing a new model car or a big company's annual staff parties would require a spectacular sendoff. This was something that Malcolm, with his partner Bob Monkhouse, specialized in. Malcolm was good to work for and — as a fellow guitarist with a significant career — was easy to talk with. The amount of music that he tried to cram into a three-hour session was not always as easy to deal with, especially for the front-line players.

Malcolm used Cy Paine to arrange all his music, be it originals or show tunes that he'd gotten clearance for. Cy would come bustling into the studio with an enormous amount of music tucked under his arm that he would proceed to give out to the assembled musicians. Malcolm Mitchell liked power music but didn't always have the power money to pay for it. This meant that the trumpets would have to play high, loud and long to help give this effect. Because of the financial restrictions, there would usually be something like two trumpets, a saxophone and a rhythm section. Nothing is worse for a trumpet player to play high, screaming notes with nothing 'under him' in the form of a trombone or a saxophone section. At the end of three hours of bash, bash, bash there was very little 'lip' left on the luckless trumpeters. Cy Paine's and Malcolm's sessions were shopped about quite a bit by the brass playing fraternity.

Cy's medleys were something to be seen. Pages and pages of music, all in a fast two, were draped across music stands, stuck to walls with tape — anything to avoid having to turn a page and the whole lot of music falling to the floor.

This reminds me of the time I was deputized for Ernie Shear with the Bill Beaumont Players for *Music While You Work* back in 1965. To those of you who can't remember the BBC Radio program, MWYW was constant music without a break for 45 minutes in the morning and 30 minutes in the afternoon. There were bands that regularly did the broadcast and were suitably equipped musically to do it. My dep. for Ernie was with this small combination that used sheet music copies that were liberally plastered with arrows and instructions as to who was going to play what and for how long and when.

Whilst setting up for the broadcast, I was introduced to the players I didn't know and presented with this enormous pile of sheet music - all placed meticulously in the order of play. Putting this pile on my music stand, I continued to plug up and tune up. As the rest of the musicians had done this broadcast many times before, they just topped and tailed the pieces whilst the pianist would jot down a few bars to modulate from one to the next. They all tacitly assumed, correctly as it happened, that I would be able to sight read the music on the live broadcast.

After the break before the show and our return to the studio, I sat nervously in my seat waiting for the Red Light. 'Here we go,' came the word from the control room and I reached for my guitar. I did not realize that a member of the band had moved my music stand so that one leg was on top of my guitar cord. Lifting my guitar to the playing position, I looked on in horror as my music stand toppled over and deposited all the music on the studio floor. Had I been allowed to pick it up by myself the music might have stayed in some sort of order. As it happened, everybody made a grab for the pieces nearest them and handed them to me -completely out of the original precise order. What a three-quarters of an hour that was! Unable to stop playing or speak throughout the broadcast, people were holding up pieces of music to tell me what was coming up next or leaning over and trying to whisper. I then had to scuffle through the pile of music, perhaps finding it at the last minute, open the pages up and sight read it. All this, and the broadcast was live!

I think that one or two incidents like mine precipitated the BBC to pre-record the broadcast. Even then there were a few big-time goofs with the tape jockey not checking that the start of the tape was actually the start of the broadcast. A couple of name bands were embarrassed to hear their false starts and the accompanying, sometimes unsavory, verbal comments go out over the air waves.

It was common for producers to bring tapes from other studios, or even other countries, to overdub an instrument or instrumental section. Then, of course, it might require two bulky and heavy tape reels to record from (very different to today's CDs in their plastic cases). One day, so legend has it, a string section was booked at Trident Studios to overdub a recording that had been made in the States. The section had been booked by an up-and-coming contractor who had just secured this connection. After a couple of times through the piece, the players realized that there was nothing extraordinary about the writing so they relaxed and the level of conversation increased. A word from the American producer to the contractor made it clear that he wasn't happy with all the chat that was going on. Silence was requested and was maintained for a few minutes. Slowly, the voices were again raised in conversation. The producer, now annoyed at the apparent disregard for his instructions, pushed down the studio talk back key and said.

'If I'm paying you American rates,' he said sternly, 'then I want the behaviour that I expect from American musicians.' (The American rates were about 75% more than the UK rates.')

Realization dawned on the players that, although the producer might be paying, they weren't getting. After some heated exchanges, the musicians got the American rate, the producer got his silence and the contractor did not get his expected 'bonus.' Many such deals went on which made contracting a lucrative business. One can just hope that it didn't happen too often.

Session musicians were involved a great deal in the backings for groups - even without George Martin's blessing. Some of the groups, who were discovered either by talent scouts or by the groups' cassettes sent to A&R men, were made up of musicians capable on their instruments but not proficient enough to record several titles in a three-hour session. Three hours was the Musicians' Union mandatory length for a recording session and some producers tried to cram as many titles as possible into that time frame. To complicate things even further, a producer could only record four backing tracks within those three hours. To avoid this, some producers (no names mentioned) would get the lead singer (or sometimes just anybody) to stand and sing the song whilst we recorded the music. This was in an effort to beat the 'backing track' ruling. In the '60s and early '70s a song or instrumental rarely lasted more than two minutes. I think 'MacArthur Park' by Richard Harris and maybe 'Grocer Jack by Mark Wirtz were the first to break the mould - or was it 'Good Vibrations'? Anyway, in theory, it was possible to record ten two-minute titles in a session, but the norm was between four and seven.

Herman's Hermits was a group signed by legendary record producer Mickie Most. He used session men to great advantage, recording many tracks for his signed artists. One half of the successful duo, the Most Brothers, he had paid his dues in show business and always knew what sounds and results he wanted in the recording studio. Mickie preferred Kingsway Studios, a studio, as the name suggests, located in Kingsway, a legendary and difficult-to-park-in main thoroughfare of London, adjacent to the Strand. It was a continuing puzzle why studios were located in places where it was most difficult to park. The Mother of them all was Air Studios at Oxford Circus. My heart always fell when I saw that name in the diary with a 10.00 a.m. start next to it. By the time I had struggled through the traffic, unloaded and dumped my guitars in the elevator area, rushed out to park on a meter, hurried back to take my guitars and amplifier up to the studio, set up and lit a cigarette, it felt like I'd already done a day's work — and I hadn't played a note yet!

I remember in particular recording the song 'Silhouettes' with Herman's Hermits in the mid-sixties. Kingsway Studios was located in the basement of a building that actually had an underground parking lot. This was something new for London. The LCC — or London County Council — had the foresight, at least on this subject, to stipulate adequate parking for every new building in the London area. Congregating in a small coffee area adjacent to the studio, the booked musicians and the group would exchange a few pleasantries and then go about what ever they had to do. The group would move into the control room and the musicians into the studio. Playing the written part for the lead electric guitar whilst the members of the group stood staring at me through the control room window was a little daunting. Following the session, a copy of the recording was given to the group and away they went to learn their parts. I'm not in any way putting down those group musicians who were excellent at the job they had to do, but studio costs and the sound of the finished product were factors that had to be considered by the producer.

There have been a lot of uninformed statements about who played on what records. On many occasions, for example, I have read of recordings which I was reported to have worked on, and hadn't - and those I hadn't and had. This applies to many recording musicians of that era.

I hope that in the process of these writings I can clear up some of the misconceptions.

I worked a lot with Mickie Most and recorded with many of his artists including Lulu, Donovan and Mary Hopkins. Moving from studio to studio during the course of a day made it difficult to remember details of titles I worked on. Although, as in the case of 'Silhouettes,' the odd title does stand out. Peter and Gordon's 'World without Love' and Lulu's 'Shout' were instances of 'those' titles.

I have to mention one of my favourite musicians, pianist Nicky Hopkins. Nicky was on the same musical plane as Jimmy Page except, with his musical education, he was able to read music. An unassuming, slightly built person with a lovely personality, he was a joy to work with. Although he was never in very good health, he mustered the strength to play that roaring Rock piano that led him to work with the Rolling Stones, Jeff Beck and other top grade artists in the UK recording studios. As much as those top artists requested Nicky to tour the world, he was forced to refuse on medical grounds.

Nicky was terribly frail. He never entered a studio; he seemed to just appear, as if through the walls. On one session he was given a piano part consisting of three pages stapled together. I sat in the guitar chair directly facing the piano and watched with increasing amazement and concern as Nicky struggled to separate the pages. To help him, I went over and pulled the pages apart.

'A bit too much for me, that was,' Nicky said, a little crestfallen.

He then went on to play a stomping rhythm piano part, his head and body moving to the tempo as if possessed. I have heard on the grapevine he has passed away. That's a great loss. Nicky was never heralded as he should have been.

Many singers owed their fame and fortune to their musical directors. One soft-spoken, tall musical director who fits into this bracket was Charles Blackwell. Like all arrangers and composers, Charles wanted to write music for film. In the late 'sixties it was not easy to break into films as the studios had composers under contract. (This later translated into being ripped off.) One of the few ways for new blood to get in was through the insistence of an agent, as with John Barry and Eve Taylor when Adam Faith got his starring role, or with the lead actor or the director of the film. I'm not sure which avenue Charles followed but there he was on the podium at Pinewood Studios, baton in hand and facing a large orchestra.

As Charles was to find out, there was more to writing film music than writing film music. Bringing his baton down with an authoritative swish, the orchestra ploughed through his first cue. After correcting some notes and discussing a few points, we were ready to rehearse to picture. I was in a position to see both the screen and Charles. The film rolled and the music played. The film stopped and the music kept playing. The projectionist rolled back to the start and was ready to roll again and the music played. Looking up at a blank screen after cutting off the orchestra, Charles came out with the classic film music statement: 'I think we'll have to play it a bit faster.'

As it turned out, the music was good and everybody was happy even though those first few minutes were a bit tense.

Whilst in Decca Studio 2 to record some tracks with Tom Jones, the producer — Peter Sullivan — asked Tom to come over to me, sit down, and rehearse a section of 'Green, Green Grass of Home,' Tom's number-one hit in 1966. We found the spot on my music that Tom was having difficulty with. I gave him the starting note and began to lead him in. Suddenly, finding his place, Tom sang with his usual gusto - straight into my right ear! I literally jumped out of my seat. I have never heard anything that loud so close before or since. I had a ringing in that ear for a good two days.

From the same stable as Tom Jones and Engelbert Humperdinck came Gilbert O'Sullivan. All managed by the hard, Welsh, harmonica-playing Gordon Mills, little Gilbert was like a lamb in a cage of lions. His gimmick was his cap. Worn at all times in the style of the 1930s Irish working class, one wondered if he was covering a bald patch. Knowing Gordon Mills, Gilbert was probably under strict contractual orders never to take it off. He wrote great lyrics for such songs as 'Claire,' 'Alone Again' and 'Nothing Rhymed' and appeared to enjoy every minute of his piano playing and singing. In fact, he was a little difficult to stop once he got going. Big Jim and I worked on quite a few sessions with Gilbert, mostly in Decca 2 at Broadhurst Gardens, Hampstead.

At the new Olympic in Barnes I had the dubious pleasure of witnessing the clash of the titan egos: Barbara Streisand and Michel LeGrand! Streisand will always be Streisand - and you don't call yourself 'Michel the Great' for nothing. Driving past the New Olympic in Barnes in South West London one morning, the first hint I had that it was going to be a big orchestra was the amount of musicians milling about outside the studio. There was a lounge/tea room in the studio, but there was also a bakery across the street where the over spill of musicians go. Just needing an acoustic guitar, I had no need to stop and unload my gear. So I parked in a side street some distance from the studio and walked the short distance back to Olympic. I entered the studio, found my chair and had a quick look at the music. Discovering there was very little for me to play, I went across the road to the bakery for a coffee. It was there that I learned the film was *Yentl*, produced by Streisand with music composed by LeGrand.

The first cue to be rehearsed was the opening sequence of the film. The leading participants in the ensuing saga took their places: Streisand in the control room and LeGrand on the podium. This didn't last for long, but at least it was a start. The music was counted in and all was well. The picture was run to the music and all *wasn't* well. Streisand left the control room at a run. Skidding to a halt in front of Michel the Great, she shouted, 'Where's the clarinet?'

LeGrand looked down at her through his dark-rimmed glasses and asked, '*What* clarinet?' (This would have been a good time for Keith Grant's 'Hitler's marching army' in the head set, but even he chickened out with this one.)

With her arm pointing at the now-blank screen, Streisand, again shouting, said: 'When the cart comes into the square, there's a man. And the man is standing by the fountain. And he is standing by the fountain playing a clarinet. I saw him playing but I didn't hear him. Where is he?'

Again, through the same dark-rimmed glasses, by now slightly misting, came the reply: 'That is not a clarinet! It is some strange European instrument. That is why I did not cover it!'

That wasn't the answer our heroine expected or wanted to hear. At a louder volume she ordered: 'To me, it's a clarinet and I want to hear one.'

With this she stormed off back to the control room, quickly followed by His Greatness. What happened inside is known only to the chosen few but the result was a quickly written clarinet part that roughly synchronized with the picture. The musicians later told me some of the other sessions were equally as stormy. I had the luck to be booked on only one!

Rod McKuen had this thing about ukuleles and would try to work the instrument into most of his recordings. I used to hire a ukulele or borrow one for his sessions but he was never happy with the sound. ('Not what I'm used to,' he would say.) The morning of a new series of sessions, Rod, walking in with this large brown paper bag, came straight over to me and said, 'Here, Vic, play this one.' I opened the bag to discover a brand new Martin Ukulele. Rod had brought it all the way from Los Angeles so he could get the sound he 'was used to.' I have to admit, it was a very good instrument and as much as I disliked playing ukuleles, it did sound good. Comes the end of the sessions and I go to give the instrument back to Rod.

'No, you keep it,' he said. 'At least I know there's a decent instrument somewhere in London.'

Every time I saw him after that I tried to give the ukulele back but he insisted I keep it for him. I still have it, but now it's back in Los Angeles.

Rod McKuen and Vic in the New Olympic recording the music for *The Prime of Miss Jean Brodie*. The lady with all the hair is French and plays the martinot, a strange whistling instrument featured in the score.

Recording Sessions

On a John Barry film session for the Bond film *From Russia With Love*, the orchestra was ploughing through a music cue when on my part appeared a blank bar with a pause sign, the instruction 'solo' and just the chord symbol, 'Em.' The orchestra shimmered into silence. This was a solo in the *very real* sense of the word.

John looked at me and I looked back at him. 'What do you want?' I asked with fear and trepidation stabbing at my heart.

'It's a Gypsy encampment — think of something,' he responded, with that 'leave-it-to-the-player-the-royalties-are-all-mine' look in his eyes.

I asked to see the picture before I thought of anything and after a couple of takes it was in the can. That's how the gypsy encampment scene was written.

John Barry was commissioned to compose the score for *Deadfall*, a film where a bank robbery takes place during a concert in the hall next to the Bank. The score had loud timpani and brass parts that the robbers use to cover the sound of their digging. The producers wanted to make it a piece for guitar and orchestra and Barry set forth to compose a concerto!

The film was set in Spain so he had the film company hire a chateau — or whatever they're called in Spain — in Santa Margarita. He'd been there a few days when I got a call from him asking for me to go to his castle in the sun and help with the guitar scoring. I was met at the small Santa Margarita airport by a limousine and, along with my case and Spanish guitar, transported to this wonderful chateau overlooking the town of Santa Margarita and its beautiful cathedral. The castle's owner, a Count DeQuela, met me and fussed around making sure I was comfortable in my suite. *Suite already*! A spacious bedroom with a sitting room with a stunning view of the valley and mountains beyond was all mine for a few days.

John was lying on his back on a chaise lounge by the pool. His right arm was conducting an imaginary orchestra while his left hand held an elaborate stopwatch. His eyes were misty with musical emotion. Then he saw me. He explained what was needed. On a small piece of manuscript was written a sketchy musical outline. After the 'hello's' were done with and the 'how was your trip?' out of the way, he said, 'This needs to be scored for guitar — make it last about five minutes with plenty of variation and some big chords.' I scuttled off to my suite and started to work on the epic.

John, Jayne Birkin (his wife at the time) the Count and his staff made me very welcome. A dinner on the terrace in the Spanish twilight with a plate of Lobster Thermidor and delicious fresh vegetables from the chateau's garden does take a bit of beating. The wine was excellent, too. Of course, with John's tunnel vision he wouldn't countenance much opposition to his way of thinking — something I had learned from working with him for such a long time, both on the road and in the studio. Unfortunately, Jayne Birkin was of the same disposition, so some of the meal times, as well as the tranquility of some of the days and nights were interrupted by loud and meaningful dissension.

Taken with the splendor of the surroundings, John decided to buy himself a chateau. Mysteriously, the Count happened to know of several. If I learned nothing else, I learned that all Spanish Chateaus in Santa Margarita are a long way from each other, owned by men of a certain emotional orientation, and are all on the top of mountains. One we visited was actually built into the mountain — pictures hung on the granite — statues carved out of the very rock itself – it was amazing. This 'chateau hunting' led to one of their more noteworthy disagreements. Jayne wanted her own place, a place she could stamp her personality on, somewhere to decorate to her choice. His response, after a heated argument in front of me and the Count DeQuela, was for her to 'fuck off with a bucket of whitewash and build your own fucking house.'

It was at that moment I decided to retire, slightly embarrassed, to my suite.

At least the next day was peaceful and I could complete the work on the guitar score. The film came out to good reviews. One article in the *London Evening Standard* contained this quote from Renata Tarago, the solo suitarist on the film's score: 'John Barry's score is beautiful and he is master of writing for the guitar, his guitar music was a joy to play.'

C'est La Vie!

Guitarist Joe Morretti was part Scottish and part Italian — a fiery combination. His wife was part Greek and part Italian — another fiery combination. They had a close relationship that was peppered with outbursts of passion, both constructive and destructive. In an unusual occurrence, Joe turned up at EMI Studios in a taxi. He was trying to pick up all his guitars and an amplifier and hold his head at the same time.

He paid off the taxi and shook his fist at the driver as he drove out the parking lot gate. In the studio, Joe looked pale and very stressed. He also had what appeared to be a large hole in his forehead, just below the hairline.

'How did that happen?' we all asked.

'The taxi driver hit me!' Joe replied.

If that was the case, why did Joe let the driver get away? It was all very suspicious. As it turned out, just as Joe was leaving his house a terrible row had broken out over who was taking Little Joe (a productive element of their more constructive relationship) to school. To settle the argument, Joe's wife hit him with the car jack and drove off after throwing his instruments on the road. After we found out what had really happened, we let Joe keep his secret.

As a guitar player, Joe wasn't too happy at sight reading some of the more difficult parts we were sometimes confronted with. He had a delightful trick of switching on his tremolo and dampening the strings of his guitar with the palm of his hand whilst looking intently at the music page and moving his head to the rhythm of the piece. A strange wobbling, deadened, burbling sound would come from his amplifier. If he was questioned about what happened to the written notes, Joe would reply that he was trying out a new effect and did the musical director like it? This bought Joe a little time to get to grips with the part.

To underline the stress that players were under in the studio recording scene, I have to tell the story of Dave Richmond and his bass amplifier. Separate amps and speakers were in vogue and Dave prided himself on his new 'amp head,' as they were called. A large orchestra had been assembled at IBC studios and the bass and guitar had been positioned at the center of the orchestra. Halfway through the first run through of the first title, the bottom suddenly dropped out of the sound. Dave's amp had died on him. For a moment Dave's facial expression did not change. Then, as realization set in, the blood drained from his face and he turned to look at the dead amp. Lights still glowed where lights should glow, but no sound was coming from the speaker. Ceasing to play, Dave hit the amp. (By the way, this is the first thing anybody should try when electrical equipment fails.)

The orchestra stopped playing and Dave's distress became the focus of about forty people. There was an immediate and financial interest at stake — immediate, because a drama was unfolding in front of them, and financial, because it could mean overtime and more pay.

Dave started to panic. Wild-eyed, he attacked knobs, cables, wires and anything that might be the cause of this dreadful silence. He finally subsided in dejected defeat and slumped in his seat next to the amp.

The look on his ashen face told us that he was imagining his career in ruins. The engineer, Adrian Kerridge, saved the situation by coming down to the studio from the control room and trying out something new. It was called 'Direct Injection' — now lovingly known as D.I. All was well and the recording session continued.

Dave never quite trusted an amp again, but the rest of us felt more at ease knowing that D.I. was there to save the day.

Another instance of panic in the studio involved Les Hurdle, also a bass player of substance; he is famous for his 'Disco Bass Line' and his work with Donna Summer. Les had turned up at Decca 2, proudly toting his new Music Man Bass Version 3. This had 'active' electronics inside the bass to amplify and modulate the signal before it left the instrument. Well, once again, fate struck and the sound from the bass died. This time there was no amp to blame as Les was D.I'd straight into the desk. Twiddling knobs and pulling cables had no affect and the instrument remained silent. In desperation, Les unscrewed the panel on the back of the instrument and began stabbing and pulling at the complicated wiring that lay beneath. Still no sound!

As a final desperate move, Les cut all the wires, apart from those attached directly to the pick-ups, and threw the lot — including the battery — on the floor. A jack plug was ripped from the end of a cord and the wires were twisted together. The bass sprung to life.

As far as I know, the amazing new technology and its attendant wiring are still lying on the studio floor.

Musical Director Alyn Aynsworth was always a challenge to work for. First of all, he was demanding of his musicians and, secondly, he used to play guitar. I remember when Alyn took over the BBC Radio Orchestra on a five-year contract in 1968. Apathy had crept into the orchestra and Alyn was the man to bring it back to life. He requested two guitars at all times in the band and I was selected to do the second chair; Bobby Moore, the staff guitarist, was the first chair. One title Alyn arranged had a pretty-but-difficult guitar intro which was repeated a few times within the piece. Bobby scuffled his way through it, as we all would have done, playing the important notes and leaving out the bits that were difficult. I must emphasize that Bobby was a good guitarist and if he couldn't get it first time then nobody could. However, Alyn asked Bobby what was the matter with the intro and why it wasn't as he had written it.

Bobby said, 'The notes don't lie under the fingers very well.'
To which Alyn replied, "Well, they lie under mine OK. Get it right!'
Bobby never questioned one of Alyn's guitar parts again.

Anthony Newley had a big hit recording of 'Strawberry Fair.' Four acoustic guitars — Bryan Daly, Eric Ford, Ernie Shear and me — had been booked and were placed high on the back rostrum in Decca 2 Studio. The parts called for chords, in a couple of different inversions, to be strummed at a maniacal tempo with 32 beats to the measure. The tune is long with many verses and their attached choruses. After the first run through we were all exhausted — and we still had two and a half hours to go. A master plan had to be set up. It was decided amongst ourselves that at every letter in the score, one of us would rest. This was done in a clockwise direction. This was probably the first time physical phasing was introduced (and the last).

Newley kept on finding new interpretations of the lyrics so, being the artist that he was, this meant many and frequent run-throughs. No thought was given by Mr Fraser, the musical director, of the physical limitations of the human body, so the sound from the acoustic guitar arena became less and less. Again, such as happens in the face of great adversity, hysteria set in. I think it is the musician's ability to see the funny side of things that has helped them through many impossible situations. However, the record got made, and it became a hit.

The difference between digging a hole in the road and making a record like 'Strawberry Fair' is certainly not physical. The difference is that there is a slight chance of getting paid again for digging the same hole! And seeing the funny side of things was the big safety valve. There was one musical director who would insist on counting in 12/8 numbers by shouting 1, 2, 3, 4, 5, 6, 7, 8, 9, 10, 11, 12. Usually, by the time he got to 7, we were incapable of playing! Of course there was always the Italian, French or German conductor whose accents made for a few light moments.

On the subject of hysteria, a German musical director came to record his version of Disco Music at EMI. The charts were impeccably copied — every instrument had an individual folder printed with its name. The German MD strutted about the studio trying to make small talk get to know the guys. I suppose he must have been quite a nice person when he was asleep. He counted the first piece in and after four bars a few sniggers came from the large figure of Jim sitting beside me. This, of course, was all it took to start the whole band trying to hide its laughter. The music was pure 'oom pah oom pah.' Even Hitler would have had to march to it.

As the piece progressed, it became more and more impossible to play. Musicians were doubled up behind their music stands getting redder and redder in the face. To make things worse, the MD stood at the Control Room window looking into the studio with a face that resembled the Judge's at the Nuremberg trials. The MD turned from the window and rushed into the studio.

'Stop! Stop! Immediately! You vill stop!' he shouted.

The band ground to a halt. Not one of us could look him in the eye. And then this gentleman said the words that should never have been said: 'Obviously, ve do not haff ze same sense of humour.'

This was the first time I have seen musicians fall of their chairs — that early in the morning and before the pubs were open. I have to say that the engineer had not escaped the contagious laughter. He had collapsed across his consul, shoulders shaking, while he wiped tears from his eyes. As happens in these situations, after everyone had calmed down the session became very 'doomy' and we were all glad to get out of there when the time was up.

I don't think the German MD ever came back to England.

Big Jim Sullivan and I used to play chess a lot in between sessions, at tea breaks if the match was close and, sometimes — if there was nothing for the guitars to play — during the sessions. We used to place the chess board on whichever amp was between us, or maybe an upturned trash can, and make our moves when we could. I can't remember anybody getting upset that we did this; in fact, most MDs were interested in who was winning. It was mostly Jim because, like everything he did, he did with a conviction and a passion that was hard to beat. Every now and then Jim would take up a new sport or hobby. As with guitar playing and chess, these activities were not done in any half measure.

Jim got turned onto star gazing. He bought a huge telescope, a mountain of books on the subject and had a concrete pad built in the middle of his garden to ensure the telescope was immovable. There were electric motors that were geared to follow the stars across the horizon. There was a bank of filters to display the spectrum of various stars and there was a pile of thick, warm clothing that Jim use to put on as the night chill crept into his bones.

We were regaled with photos of his night's activities. Every photo looked the same to me, but he went to great lengths to explain the difference.

Then, suddenly, Jim went out and bought a wet suit. Not just any wet suit. This one was fitted to his body like a second skin. He bought the latest in oxygen bottles, masks, flippers, compasses, depth gauges, watches that would work hundreds of feet below the surface, weight belts, under water cameras, lights. He put all this gear on, abandoning his telescope and concrete pad, and dove into a waterlogged gravel pit near his home in north London. Just once, that was all!

The gear is still in a closet somewhere because immediately after surfacing Jim discovered the sitar and Ravi Shankar… And then meditation… And then…

As much as there were stressful times in studios, there were very pleasant and happy times. Henry Mancini would come across from the States to record a film or make an album for Readers Digest. A more pleasant person no one could wish to work with. An excellent pianist, composer and arranger, his charts were always a pleasure to play. From the small groups he sometimes used on *The Pink Panther* films to the large orchestras for his films and albums, there was always some musical delight to look forward to. 'Hank,' as he was familiarly known, would be playing a piano solo and drop a clam.

'Hell,' he would say, 'you guys are better off without me.'

In one instance when he was conducting from the piano, he said, 'Stop that chord when I jerk off the piano.' When he realized the connotation of what he had said, Hank was incapable of playing for quite a few minutes.

It takes a great man to laugh at himself.

Bryan Daly was a guitar player I worked with a great deal over the years. He was quite a character: He imagined himself as part of the British landed gentry. Not an impossible task as he cut an impressive figure. When we were continually doing three sessions a day, Bryan would often say, 'I'm far too tired to work in the morning; no gentleman should be expected to work in the afternoon, and the evening is for taking a leisurely dinner at my club.'

One session at CTS, where we were working together, the two guitars weren't required on a particular piece of music. I wandered up to the control room to have a listen and maybe chat with the sound engineer, John Richards, while Bryan remained in his chair. The sessions had been going well and everyone was in good spirits. I can't remember his name but the producer knew Bryan well and, peering out the control room window, noticed him with his head back, fast asleep, his guitar leaning against a sound screen. We were all called to the window to look at Bryan who was by now well into Never-Never land. With a wicked grin, the producer turned to John and told him to ask to hear Bryan's guitar part, which, of course, he didn't have. John pressed the talk-back button and said in a commanding voice: 'Bryan Daly, let me hear your guitar from letter "A."'

This was the first time we had all ever witnessed panic in slow time. As Bryan's head slowly came forward, his left hand automatically felt for his guitar. At the same time as his unfocused eyes tried to find the music, he pulled the guitar onto his lap and started to play anything. He looked desperately from my music stand to his to find out what he should be playing. Realizing there was no guitar part he looked up at the control room window to see a row of laughing faces. I think it took a good part of his British landed Gentry image to stop him doing something drastic to us all. We laughed many times about that incident — once he found out it wasn't my idea!

I was sitting in front of a percussionist one day who wasn't making his part. His confusion was made more apparent as I had exactly the same phrase to play and the unison wasn't unison! After several tries, with the conductor becoming more annoyed, I turned round and confronted his red face which, at the time, had a large cigar sticking out of it. Sarcastically I said, 'Shall we play it your way or how it's written?'

Now, I have often wondered what goes on in people's minds when they are in a 'back-against-the-wall' situation. The reply given to me by Bobby Midgley — for that was his name — didn't stop me wondering.

'It's alright for you to just sit there,' he spluttered. 'I've got to fix a rhythm section for Buckingham Palace.'

To this very day, I laugh about that when I think of it.

Professionals in any field make their work seem easy but, underneath the calm exterior that the public sees can be a hidden turmoil. Arranger and musical director Arthur Greenslade was a seasoned professional. His work with American singer and poet, Rod McKuen, can attest to that. Before one of Arthur's and Rod's sessions — it may well have been for the film *The Prime of Miss Jean Brodie* — Judy and I were visiting Arthur and his wife Eileen. Inviting me into his study, Arthur said, 'Listen to this cassette I've just received from McKuen.'

He pressed the play button on his tape recorder and after a short silence there came some erratic whistling followed by comments such as, 'That's when she enters the school' and, 'Make this last about four minutes.' The musical phrase that McKuen had whistled was barely ten seconds long. Arthur, being who and what he was, had to sit down and make that whistle into four minutes of music to be played by a sixty-piece orchestra.

Arthur was also the Musical Director for Engelbert Humperdinck, a good singer whom I have known for years and years, even before he was Engelbert. 'Enge,' as he likes to be called now, can, like many other singers, be very demanding. Because the arrangements were always good and on time, our Enge would ask Arthur to come up with a new arrangement, or an arrangement of a new song, sometimes as quickly as for the next day's afternoon rehearsal — and this request would come just before that night's performance.

Arthur's nerves couldn't stand this continual stress and he became seriously ill. Another factor that didn't help Arthur's condition was that previous to working with Enge, he had been musical director to Shirley

Bassey. Having worked with Miss Bassey on records, television and concerts, I can only wonder how there was anything left of Arthur to work for Humperdinck! Anyway, Arthur had a complete nervous breakdown and one of the unpleasant side effects was that his skin started to fall off. Being warned by his doctors that his body and his nervous system couldn't take any more, Arthur retired and went to live with his daughter in Australia. He is now a happy man and plays piano when and where he wants to. (Good on yer, cobber!)

Arthur was musical director on BBC Radio's *Saturday Club*. Featured with one or two instrumental numbers with his 'G Men,' they were mainly booked to accompany the endless succession of singers that were going up and down the hit parade. The radio show proved very popular and was repeated many times by the BBC both during the time it was running and in later years. The musicians who worked on the show were supposed to get a residual fee every time it was repeated, but somehow we never did. Arthur purchased a beautiful home in the suburbs of London which boasted six bedrooms, billiard room and even a small dance hall. There was a rumour that Arthur was going to call it 'Repeat House'!

On that touchy subject, Charlie Katz was once asked why he didn't pay out repeats. His answer: 'It costs too much.'

To add some depth to Charlie's answer, I was booked for a series by BBC Radio to supply a quintet to play incidental music for the BBC Radio 2's *Concert Hour*. There were Eric Ford, Judd Procter, Dave Richmond, John Dean, and myself. We recorded about six Latin-American-style titles in one session, which amounted to nearly twenty minutes of music. These recordings were repeated and I received some very nice cheques from the BBC, thank you very much. Dividing the amount by five, I mailed off the money to the musicians. Eric Ford called me one day and asked what all the money was for. I told him it was his share of the repeat money I had received. Now Eric has probably done more broadcasts than most people have had hot dinners, so what he said next holds a wealth of meaning: 'I've never had a repeat cheque this big from anybody.'

Nothing more needs to be said!

No matter how good a musician or conductor a person may be, for some, the technical side of the recording business seems to elude them. John Pearson was both an excellent pianist and composer (*News at 10* theme), but whose comprehension of the technical side finished when the sound left the instrument. Being musical director of the long running BBC TV show, *Top of the Pops*, led to John having to deal with (for him) the most formidable of all opponents, the Metronome. John was paranoid about getting the right tempo for the various artists the orchestra was backing. If the acts were segue, it was an education to look up from my music stand to observe John conducting in one tempo and trying to establish the tempo of the next act on his Metronome. That is, if he had managed to switch it on. He would glare at it, tap it on the podium, mutter strange ritual incantations into the little speaker, all whilst still waving his hand to conduct the orchestra. As the current number drew to a close, Johnny's panic increased. Oblivious as to what was going on around him, he was brought back to reality by recognition of the ending musical phrases. Somehow, the show went smoothly and nobody ever did complain about tempos.

Headsets were another of John's stumbling blocks. One day at Olympic, the music that John had written needed more adjustments than usual due to a temperamental producer. Some producers/directors were firmly of the opinion that they could write a better musical score than any composer and would try to alter the music to how they 'heard' it. Forced to move about the studio floor at a rapid rate, John had pulled the headset connection apart. This in itself must have hurt John as we all saw his head jerk as the cable broke. Not connecting the pain with the loss of sound, John continued altering the music whilst constantly banging the headset in a vain effort to make them work. The headset was now perched at a ridiculous angle on his head. Keith Grant, with a bird's eye view of the hilarious situation, could hardly speak, and was relaying the producer's instructions as best he could over the playback speakers. Of course, with the headset on, John was unable to hear the speakers clearly. All efforts to tell John of his predicament failed so we were left to watch this frenzied, gesticulating figure wandering about the studio, banging his head. The significant length of cable which trailed behind him got caught up in microphone and music stands.

Cruel as it is to say so, it's moments like that that made the job so wonderful.

John was an excellent pianist and would often write impossible things for himself to play. On broadcasts you could see his hands fluttering over the keys in a last-minute silent rehearsal. The performance was always impeccable. It was on one of John's broadcasts at BBC Piccadilly 1 that I introduced a 'new sound' to the world of broadcasting: a Fuzz Box. Suggesting to John that I used it on an electric guitar solo passage, I plugged it in and the orchestra played the number. Before we had finished, the producer burst out of the control room door and starting shouting from the gallery.

'What the Devil was that awful noise where the guitar solo was?' (Remember he was a BBC producer!)

'It was a Fuzz Box,' John said, and with all innocence, added, 'I quite like it.'

'I don't care what it's called and I don't care what you like. I will not have distortion on the BBC,' the producer ranted.

After hearing groups like 'The Who' on record and shows like the BBC's *Top of The Pops*, I imagine that our producer has taken to the hills or the furthest monastery, never to be seen again.

John Pearson and John Schroeder were the brains behind 'Sounds Orchestral' who, in February of 1965, had a top ten hit with 'Cast Your Fate to the Wind.' Instrumental hits are very hard to follow so there was a desperate search for the 'Sounds Orchestral' next single. Working with John Pearson and John Schroeder on a different artist's session, I played a piano number to them that I had composed and, to my surprise, they loved it. To my further amazement it became the next single release of 'Sounds Orchestral.' I was all set for the giddy heights of a successful songwriting career. Unfortunately, the public didn't have the same rapturous enthusiasm that Mr Pearson and Mr Schroeder had, there were also contractual bickerings going on so the record company didn't 'work' the record. Although getting a lot of plays on the radio, my brain child, 'A Boy and a Girl' didn't make the charts.

This was similar, in a way, to the experience I had with the disc jockey Tony Blackburn's singing career. Tony was looking for a song to make his mark on the British public and to thumb his nose, in a good natured way, at the other disc jockeys' habit of making fun of his singing. Through Les Reed's Publishing Company (Donna Music), one of my songs was presented to Tony and he liked it! With a few alterations in the lyrics by Barry Mason, of 'Deck Chair' fame, Tony Blackburn recorded the song. It was released to a fanfare of publicity and because of their previous joking about Tony's singing, nearly all the radio disc jockeys constantly played the record. It started selling like hot cakes.

Once again, I was set for the big time. The sales department and everybody connected with the record were jumping up and down. This has got to be it, I thought. What could possibly happen to stop this record going to the top of the charts? A six-week strike at the EMI pressing plant is what happened — and the record died. And, for a while, so did my faith in humanity. I was starting to be convinced that all the successful record producers, songwriters and singers had a direct line to God and that I just wasn't privy to his personal number.

Wally Ridley was an A&R man at EMI. Very precise and always immaculately dressed, Wally was very much of the 'old school'. Everything had to be prepared well in advance. He would expect the orchestra to be sitting down and tuned up for the start of the session and expected the first down beat to happen as the second hand clicked to the top of the hour. Bring into this scenario an arranger by the name of Johnny Keating and the consequences proved funny, sad and embarrassing all at the same time.

Keating was responsible for many of the Ted Heath big band charts but, great arranger that he was, he had this penchant for always leaving things to the last minute. This particular day we were all seated and tuned and waiting for Johnny Keating to arrive. Wally was pacing up and down and frequently looking up at the studio clock. Five minutes after the scheduled start of the session, Johnny came rushing through the double doors at the end of the studio clutching some scores and some parts. Apologizing to Wally for being late, Johnny hurriedly moved through the orchestra distributing parts. Wally always liked to have a copy of the score for his use in the control room. The first hint that all was not well was when Johnny confessed to not having a copy of the score for the first number. If you had forgotten something or played a wrong note, you didn't apologise to Wally, you confessed your sins in as humble a manner as possible. In a slight huff, Wally listened to the first run-through before ascending the stairs to the control room. After a few rehearsals and a couple of takes, the first number was in the can. A perfunctory 'thank you' preceded Wally's descent down the studio stairs for the same ceremonies at the start of the second number. Johnny distributed the parts to many fewer members of the orchestra than for the first tune. Looking at the part in front of me, I knew this wasn't going to be a happy day. All it had on it was the title. No music. Just the title!

Johnny counted in and nothing happened. I shall never forget his desperate words: 'Come on Fellas. Don' make me work,' his soft Scottish accent lending an added drama to the moment.

'What's wrong, John?' Wally inquired, sensing that this wasn't going to be his finest hour.

Johnny went into a huddle with Wally and the two of them went up the stairs to the control room. The studio speakers clicked and Wally's voice proclaimed: 'That's all for today. Thank you.'

We couldn't get out of that studio and the terrible atmosphere quick enough. Thank goodness that was the only time I personally witnessed such an event.

It was in EMI Studio 1 that a warning light came on for me. Booked to just play one electric guitar solo line for a film score written by Ken Thorne, I set up quietly in an isolation booth as the orchestra rehearsed and recorded the cue before the one I was in. The cue now in the can, Ken turned to see if I was all set. Smiling a 'hello' to me, he turned and counted in the orchestra. Coming to my solo, all was well until about eight bars in. I made to play a note with my third finger and nothing happened. The finger didn't move. I was telling it to — but it didn't move. Fortunately, the melody line at that point was slow and I just had time to slide up with my second finger and play the note. I broke out into a cold sweat and the room started to move around me. Recovering slightly, I tried to move the finger. It responded slowly. Somehow I managed to play, and record that cue, without using the third finger of my left hand.

That moment happened in 1979 and on two other occasions that finger was slow to react. I consulted my doctor and he had all the tests run and, happily, these proved everything was OK. As it turns out, it was a combination of stress, over-use and age. The condition is not that uncommon and has been given a name — 'Constant Use Syndrome' — at least I *think* that's what it's called. In my case, I personally think it was Constant *Over*-Use Syndrome, resulting in fatigue and deterioration.

I was the arranger on a recording at Phillips for an independent label which was being produced by Tommy Sanderson. Tommy had been around the business for years. Pianist accompanist for many famous singers, Tommy had found himself in music publishing working for Francis Day and Hunter as Manager of their Pop Music section. He also dabbled as a manager, a fact that cost me several hundred pounds in unpaid invoices.

On this particular session at Phillips, I had booked Reg Guest on piano. Reg was another fine pianist and underrated arranger, although he could be a little temperamental and could react quickly to criticism, and not always in the nicest way. Tommy had come out the control room and was asking Reg to play in a certain style that Tommy thought suited the tune. Tommy then tried to show Reg what he wanted. Wrong move! Suddenly, Reg had little Tommy pinned against the wall with his arm, still sitting at the piano, mind you, and said in a controlled but angry voice, 'I don't need you to show me. I know what you want!'

Tommy turned a strange colour but managed to restrain himself, no doubt thinking of the effect any kind of outburst would have on the success of the session. Such incidents, though few and far between, do leave a nasty taste. I further annoyed Reg on the same session by playing something he couldn't. Reg was trying to play ascending and descending octaves perfectly together. He just couldn't get it to work. Reg got up as I was passing so I sat at the piano and with more luck than skill played the octaves perfectly, first time. To have this happen, especially by a guitar player, and on top of the incident with Tommy Sanderson, was too much for Reg. He went into a severe depression and would only speak when spoken to for the rest of the session.

I mentioned that Tommy Sanderson was little. He was more 'small' than little. His hair was permanently over his eyes, and his chin had a blue tint to it; he was fondly nicknamed 'The Burglar.' Many musicians had nicknames. Some knew it, some didn't. A wonderful sax and flute player, Roy Willox, was nicknamed 'The Policeman.' Roy, good naturedly, entered into the fun of the thing. It was amusing to see Tommy and Roy talking together which they did on the odd occasion and, for a joke, Roy would 'frog march' Tommy out the studio if he was making too many waves. Other nicknames like 'The Silk Stocking Murderer,' 'The Caterer' and 'The Olympic Drummer' (because he always seemed to be trying to get to the end of the arrangement before anybody else) were well known. Pianist and musical director, Johnny Arthey — sometimes known as Paul Windsor — thought his nickname was something other than what it actually was. At a party at his house, he said: 'I know what my nickname is. The boys call me "The Captain."' There were a few hidden smiles from the musicians present.

Sorry you've been under a delusion all these years, Johnny. How does 'The Corporal' sound?

Still, a bit of self promotion never hurt anybody. I could be wrong, like Johnny Arthey, but I think mine was 'The U Boat Commander.' Blonde hair combined with my last name? Who knows?

I just hope it wasn't 'Sailor'!

During this period American musicians arriving and working in the UK were few and far between. One reason was the reciprocal Musicians' Union ruling that for an American musician to work in the UK a UK musician had to either go to the States or a UK musician had to be paid the same as the American musician and not play. Promoters were reluctant to pay twice for one performance, especially if it meant a sixteen-piece band.

Luckily, some did manage to get with the program and worked in jazz clubs, concert halls and studios. Billy Cobham was imported from the USA by international contractor Nat Peck to work on some film sessions. Of course, I can't remember the film or the composer, but I do remember Billy, a drummer with an impressive discography. He was known mainly for his 'fusion' work. However, on these sessions all the music cues were worked with a click track, something that appeared to be new to Billy. His expansive and complicated drum kit was set up in the main isolation booth in Studio One, CTS. The large orchestra with its six or seven piece rhythm section — which includd Martin Kershaw and me on guitars--was ready to play. Within a few bars, things started to go wrong. Even though the click track was meant to hold everything together, Billy very soon started to go adrift. In his defense, being tied to a click track can be very demanding if the music has complicated rhythms, which, as I remember this cue did, and if Billy was used to playing free form, then his job became even more arduous.

The music cue ground to a halt and discussions began between the conductor, Billy and Nat Peck. Martin and I put in a discreet request to John Richards in the control room for the isolated drums to be taken out of the head sets. The next run-through and the rest of the sessions went fine with just the occasional muffled sound escaping from the booth. Following those couple of days I bought a recording with Billy Cobham. He does play some amazing drums – presumably without a click track.

Another American drummer I held in awe was Louie Bellson, so imagine my excitement when I got a call from Eric Delaney's manager, Derek Bolton, to work a couple of sessions for their 'Repercussions' album at EMI 2 with Eric and Louie. I always had the impression that Louie was one heavy hitter as a drummer. From his solos and his big band work, I wasn't sure where a guitar was going to fit in. In the studio everything was different. First of all, Louie was the most likeable and mild-mannered person you could wish to meet and Eric was the epitome of the dapper, well-dressed 'man about town.' Indeed, looking at Eric and Louie just talking together made it difficult to imagine they were both such powerhouse percussionists. The sessions were very enjoyable with saxophonist Alan Skidmore, trumpeter Tony Fisher and tuned percussionist Jim Lawless amongst the impressive lineup.

One of the biggest emotional highs I experienced in my music career happened in 1984. It was not with a swinging rhythm section or an orchestra — in fact I was, in essence, part of the audience. A small rhythm section had been booked by Ivor Raymond to travel from London to Rhos (a small town in Wales) to record an album of Jim Reeves' country hits with the Rhos Male Voice Choir. Arriving at the small town, we made our way to the school and into the large hall where the sound engineers had set up their equipment. Just before the first session of the day, we could look out into the body of the hall from our position seated on the stage and see the members of the choir as they filed in and took up their singing formation. Like any choir, or any group of people for that matter, the choristers came in all shapes and sizes. It has always surprised me that some of the deepest voices came from the thinnest and smallest of men. All these men, from every walk of life, seemed a little nervous as we were being introduced as 'the excellent and famous musicians from London who traveled all this way to accompany us.'

Perhaps what the choir master said wasn't quite true, but I was prepared to believe him. He was a small, wiry man with a contagious enthusiasm and love for choral music. It was evident that this choir was his life and in the course of attaining perfection he actually bullied his choristers, some of whom were twice his size. All responded to his commands with a respectful fear. Shouting at them, if their performance wasn't up to the standard he expected, he singled out individual singers for their own personal tirade if they weren't paying enough attention, or for bad intonation. Now and again he would give out praise in the manner of royalty bestowing a knighthood — and that praise was received and coveted with as much pleasure as if it were a knighthood. All the songs on the album had been made famous by Jim Reeves, the acclaimed American country singer. To my mind not all of the songs were suitable for a large choir — too many words sung too quickly by too many people, but the overall effect was very good. The choir had rehearsed their parts for weeks and was nearly perfect. This helped us to record the whole album in the one day we were there. Praise must also go to Ivor for the arrangements and the organization. An added tension to the day's work was the very real threat of there being no electricity at 4 p.m. The coal miners had called a national strike and to conserve electricity, the National Grid was to be shut down at selected times in selected areas. To obtain the greatest effect, the miners had chosen winter time for their industrial action, when, of course, the need for power was the greatest.

The morning session went very well with over half of the titles being recorded. A lunch break was called at noon when the warm hospitality of the Welsh people embraced us and we were driven of by the 'lads' to their local pub. Thinking the 'local' would be local we were surprised to be driven away from the school, away from the town, down winding lanes until we reached our destination — a small public house in an idyllic setting. Nestling at the foot of a steep hill with a fast running stream at the side of the car park, the pub was all we expected it to be.

'Why is your local so far away?' we asked the choir master.

In the broadest of Welsh accents he replied, 'It wouldn't do to be caught drinking in the town — what would our parents think?'

Amazingly, the majority of the choristers were middle-aged and they were still cautious of what their parents might think of them. Inside the pub, some twenty to thirty members of the choir had gathered in the various bars to enjoy their 'lunch.' Thick crusty home made bread and meat pies all washed down with the excellent local brew. There was a public bar, a lounge bar (the one with the padded chairs), a snug bar, a private bar and a small section for 'off sales.' This is where alcoholic beverages could be sold to unidentifiable people through a hatch cut in a side door.

'Some people don't like it known they take a drink,' came the plausible straight-faced explanation.

Although everybody knew who did what, when and where, nobody knew — if you know what I mean.

Quietly, through the conversation and the clatter of knives, forks, glasses and the cash register could be heard a single voice singing the opening notes from the choir's repertoire. The voice stilled the noises in the pub and one by one the men joined in. Within less than thirty seconds, the whole gathering was singing with an unconcealed passion. I have to tell you, bread, butter, cheese and a pint of beer never tasted better — especially when washed down with tears. The moment ended as quickly as it had begun as the men realized they had to drive back and finish the recording. We continued with the recording until, as promised by the local Electricity Board, the lights went out at exactly 4 p.m. Fortunately, even with one number left to record, there was enough material on tape to make an album.

With the lights in the hall now extinguished and the early winter twilight softening everyone's focus, the choir master turned to us and said, 'The Choir would like to sing for you, as an expression of our thanks, the song that gave us first place in "The National Eisteddfod."'

This was the culmination of all the local Eisteddfods — or music festivals — that had been held in Wales during the previous year. To be champions was an honor to be cherished. As the choir master spoke to us, the members of the choir began to light candles, and in the warm soft glow I became aware of an absolute quiet. A low, pianissimo passage gradually became a swelling crescendo as the singers threw their hearts into the performance. The choir of one hundred men seemed to become a single living entity. The wondrous sound rose up from the floor of the hall to envelope us, to surround us, to enter our very souls. I was completely overcome. With tears rolling down my face, I could just about see out over the heads of the choir, through the large hall windows to the soft dark blue outline of Welsh mountains, almost invisible in the twilight. What a glorious moment! How privileged I was to have been there.

The standard of musicianship shown by all the studio players was incredibly high. The musical director used to hand round the parts, count the title in and it would come out perfect first-time round. Some visiting arrangers would be a little skeptical of our musical abilities and talk through the arrangements (pointing out difficult parts etc.) then be amazed at the instant performance we would give. The guitarists at that time were some of the greatest guys I could wish to meet — Eric Ford, Jim Sullivan, Jimmy Page, John McLaughlin, Judd Proctor, Bryan Daly and Joe Morreti.

In the earlier days there was a good spirit of camaraderie that somehow got lost as the seriousness of the financial element and the whiz kids with the unending ability to redo their parts on separate tracks took over. Many are the studios that have echoed to the cry: 'It'll be OK, I'll do it again on a separate track' as the 'flavor of the month' stumbled through his part.

I have not been without my share of traumas in the studio. My colleagues and I used to suffer from an affliction known affectionately as 'the red mist.' This mist used to slowly obliterate the vision as one realized one wasn't going to make the part — or the part was so difficult that something akin to advanced stage fright set in. I remember a session for Alyn Aynsworth at EMI where the ability to play guitar seemed to completely desert me, just when I needed it the most. Alyn was a most demanding musical director and this session was one of the first in his contract with EMI. The importance of this moment can be underlined by the fact that Alyn had sold up and moved from Manchester, in the North of England, to London on the strength of his newfound career opportunity — an opportunity that was fast disappearing when seen through my eyes, even as blurred as they were becoming. The basis of the instrumental piece was a tricky little phrase played by the guitar and then repeated by the string section. It would be opportune to note at this stage that music written for strings, violins, cellos etc., is not always easily played on another instrument. I think Alyn had written the piece as a string feature and then, to 'modernize' it, had added the guitar solo. Anyway, what he had written on this particular occasion had me beat. My fingers, eyes, brain and every other part of my body that was needed to perform this piece went into total freeze mode.

Of course the whole traumatic experience was compounded by Alyn Aynsworth's attitude toward me as the session progressed. What had been 'hail fellow, well met' was quickly becoming 'get the hell out of my life.' After many, many stops and starts, the tune and the session ground to its finality. Alyn was furious, the musicians were thanking God it wasn't them, and, on the inside, I was a blubbering wreck. On the outside, however, I was still trying to maintain an air of professional aloofness. I have to admit that I got in my car, drove to a quiet street and cried my heart out. It made me feel better, but it was a long time before Alyn used me again. Interestingly, not one of the musicians on that session ever brought up that embarrassing incident in conversation, and I worked with them all for many years after. Perhaps it was because every musician knows that his Waterloo is just a 'phone call and a few notes away.

My return to the Aynsworth fold came when I turned up at a session at Chappells in Bond Street. Entering the studio, Alyn and I locked eyes. It was not a good moment. Having struggled back up his reputation ladder following our last meeting, I could sense Alyn's fear of returning to the bottom rung. Obviously, this was a case of the contractor having tried everybody else that was warm and, through the fickle fortunes of fate, had booked me. The music was for a TV show — the usual mixture of medleys and backing tracks for singers. However, there was one number that I had espied during my quick reconnoiter through the pad and this looked anything but usual. I had nothing to lose. When the time came to rehearse the title, I played well. There was an eight-measure solo in the middle which I covered easily. Alyn still hadn't looked my way again since our first encounter. When the take came, I let it go. I screamed up and down the fret board with complete abandon. Strings bent like elastic bands, distorted dissonance cascading from my amp. I put it all into those eight bars. And I received the accolade I had waited years for, a wisp of a smile, the faintest nod of Alyn Aynsworth's head.

I've had my fair share of embarrassing moments, some of which have been *so* embarrassing that I have felt physically sick. It's also very difficult to sit through other people's embarrassing moments. There's nothing you can do to help, so you just feel for them and hope things will get better. Consider Basil Kirchin, a wonderful drummer. Instead of using a drum stool, Basil had fixed a comfortable touring bicycle seat on to the regular metal tripod. When he played — which he normally did with great enthusiasm — he would balance himself on this bicycle seat, his arms and legs seeming to have a life of their own as they lashed out at bass drums, cymbals, tom toms and snare drum. What an inspiring sight that was! I've only worked with him once, and that was with a big orchestra in Kingsway Hall, but I have heard him and seen him and have always been very impressed. Of course, the only other time I was directly involved with Basil was when we were on opposing sides in the Marty Wilde fiasco at the Regal, Edmonton.

Basil Kirchin is also a composer. One day at Denham Film Studios a large orchestra was assembled for six sessions to record the music for a film. Basil had composed the music and much of the orchestration had been done by John Coleman. Neither of those two good gentlemen will thank me for reminding them of this incident, but it has to be documented. After the usual preliminaries, the orchestra was counted into the first cue. A brash, beautifully orchestrated piece of music was the result. Strident trumpets, a frantic rhythm section, untamed strings. All seemed to struggle for supremacy right up to the last chord. After a few seconds, numbing silence the director exited the confines of the control room and strode purposefully toward Basil and John. A deep discussion ensued, accompanied by some animated gesticulating. It was obviously decided to try the cue once more, this time to the picture. I was in the position to be able to see the footage as I played my part.

A demure-looking girl on a mild-looking horse was trotting gently across what appeared to be a golden meadow. The strident trumpets, frantic rhythm section and untamed strings followed her progress across the screen until, with the last exuberant chord, she disappeared from view. Unfortunately for Basil, the director didn't disappear with her. Very red and very angry, he again forced our luckless musician into a deep, and this time, loud discussion. With a crash of his hand on the podium the director shouted, 'I don't care what you thought. I want a fucking tune! Just give me a simple fucking tune for Chris' sake!'

It was clear that diplomatic relations had reached an all-time low.

The tormented group of adversaries moved like a rugby football scrum to the piano at which desperate attempts were made to compose a melody that would satisfy the enraged director. Nothing worked. The director returned to the control room with one of those 'looking at the floor' walks, and called for the contractor. Once more, a lengthy discussion took place after which the orchestra was given a fifteen-minute break. The outcome was that Basil's services were no longer required. However, the director insisted that the orchestra fulfill the booking. Even stranger and quite unprecedented, he sent out to various publishing houses for standard arrangements of his favorite titles and made us record them. He was in the position of having to pay for the orchestra and he was going to make us work, and work we did, right up to the very last minute. Basil and John weren't the first to have their work discarded and they won't be the last. They should be pleased, in a backhanded sort of way, to have joined John Barry, David Whittaker and others in the ranks of some of the most famous and prolific composers who have had their work rejected — but it still must have been awful for them all. The salt in the wound was that it happened in front of their peers.

The Readers Digest sessions hold many memories for me. Apart from the two sessions I composed, arranged and conducted, the others gave many opportunities to talk and relate tales of the business. A favorite story teller was Frank Horrox, a prolific session pianist and longtime member of the Ted Heath Orchestra. Frank had a history of being accident prone. A classic story of his never fails to make me laugh whenever I think of it...

Frank arrived home early from a gig and decided to surprise his wife. Creeping into the house, he looked about the ground floor, kitchen and living room and not finding her, he crept up the stairs. Opening the bedroom door as quietly as he could (this is not going to be what you are thinking), he found his wife in front of the wardrobe hanging up a dress on a wire coat hanger. He walked silently toward her and gave out with a 'BOO!' She freaked out. Whipping round with the hanger in her hand, she pierced Frank's nose. Frank howled in agony. Once the initial pain had subsided to a bearable level, any effort to remove the offending hanger or even take the dress off resulted in excruciating agony. The only way to remove the hanger and the dress was to deaden Frank's nose. This meant a trip to the hospital. Frank was led gently down the stairs, out the front door and into the car for his trip to the Emergency Room. As Frank related, to have a dress on a hanger suspended from your nose was embarrassing enough. Embarrassing also when sat in a car, suffering the amazed looks of other drivers and passengers. But try walking the length of a hospital waiting room in the same condition!

Another Frank story...

The Horrox family liked to go camping. One night they set up a tent in a field outside a small village in the North of France and bedded down for the night. In the small hours of the morning, a storm threatened to blow the tent down so Frank crept out in the pouring rain and secured the tent to the bumper of the car. (They had bumpers in those days.) Waking later to a bright and still morning, Frank decided to go get some groceries from the local village. Jumping in his car, he sped off down the road — dragging the entire tent with him. The family wasn't at all surprised!

And one more...

Frank was known for his imitation of Jimmy Durante looking for the 'lost chord.' He would grab an empty cup and, holding it between his teeth to imitate Durante's 'schnozzola,' and go into the 'Dat's not da chord! Dat ain't da one either!' routine.

Sitting at the piano with a solo passage to play, Frank started to do his Durante routine just as the conductor called the Readers Digest orchestra to order ready for the take. In an effort to finish his routine, Frank grabbed the nearest cup and thrusting it between his teeth, covered his face, shirt and jacket in hot coffee — just as the baton came down. It was another one of those times when it is very difficult to play and see the music with tears in your eyes from suppressed laughter.

Dear Frank. He was a legend.

Feeling ill was not an accepted excuse for not turning up at a recording session. Being hospitalized or maybe dying had more impact but both contingencies were still frowned upon by most of the fixers/contractors — there was always the suspicion that you were trying to get out of a date to do a more lucrative one. Having to go to Germany for Syd Dale's Music Company one year came at a time when I was feeling particularly bad but not ill enough to cancel. After all, I was still breathing and slightly warm!

Syd had started the very successful Library Music Company and because of a musicians' union ruling that no music intended for background or library music could be recorded in the UK, many companies like Syd's were going abroad. To ensure the quality of musicianship that he was used to and also to be able to work with at least a few familiar faces, Syd would take a small rhythm section and maybe a soloist to Germany for his recordings. Along with Jim Lawless, Gerry Butler, Dave Richmond, and John Dean, I had been booked to do five days' recording at Munich's Bell Studios. Two days before flying to Germany, I knew that I had got some cold or flu virus. Feeling lethargic and suffering from alternate bouts of hot sweats and shivering, I was dreading making any kind of trip let alone flying to Germany and working at a pretty hectic pace for five days.

The morning of the flight I was feeling a little better and decided, against my better judgment, to make the trip. A strange side affect of the malaise that lurked within me was a dull aching in my left leg. Judy made a quick diagnosis of a pulled muscle and liberally applied some sort of balm on my leg. At first my leg felt better, but on the drive to the airport the shivering and hot sweats started again and my leg began to feel most peculiar. Covered with liniment my leg felt hot on the outside and freezing cold on the inside. A few minutes later, the reverse happened, and so on until we reached the airport. Feeling dreadful and with this strange-feeling leg, I started to wish I'd canceled. As it was too late now to do anything about it, I staggered from the car clutching electric and acoustic guitars plus my suit case and made my way to join the rest of the group on the plane.

Liberal doses of whisky from the flight attendants helped dull the sensations but at the same time it gave Syd good reason to give me one or two old-fashioned 'looks.' I got through the first day of recording by using all the energy and will power I could muster. Returning to the rather bleak hotel, I went straight to bed after taking some non-prescription medicine to help me sleep. Next morning found me incapable of getting out of bed. I called Syd and told him it was no use, I'd had it. He'd have to go on without me to the studio.

'Get me a doctor before I die.' I pleaded.

An hour later a prim-looking middle-aged woman was let into my room by one of the hotel staff. She introduced herself as the doctor and asked for my symptoms. I told her about everything, including my leg, and after taking my pulse and temperature she declared, 'You haff und virus.'

I could have told her that.

She continued in her best 'B-movie' English: 'Vot is your name, pleez, for ze prescription?'

'Flick. Victor Flick,' came my hushed, semi-delirious reply.

The doctor stopped writing and looked up. On hearing my name, her attitude had immediately changed from one of sympathy to cold detachment.

'Flick, did you say?'

'Yes. What's the matter?' I mumbled.

She lowered her voice and said in an icy tone, 'Don't mention your name loudly around zees parts. It eez not goot!'

My concern was rising with my temperature. My eyes wide with apprehension as I asked: 'What's wrong with my name? Tell me what's wrong.'

'Herr Mick Flick, ze multi-millionaire, has sold most of his shares in a big munitions factory and a lot of people haff lost zeir monies. He is not popular. Pleez remain quiet viz your name.'

Perhaps it was the fever that helped imprint these details indelibly on my memory. It was like being in a horror film. I have to admit that on top of my fever I was starting to feel frightened. Here I was, in a cold, sparsely furnished German hotel room home many miles away and my only friends working in a studio I knew not where. And this dispassionate Teutonic woman is telling me to be secretive about my name. Again, perhaps it was the fever, but I was starting to hear goose-stepping soldiers and the rattle of half-tracks in the wide deserted streets of suburban Munich... 'They' were coming for me!

'Here. Take zis pill. I vill send ze hotel for ze ozzers.'

The female 'camp commandant' handed me a glass of water and a pill. I swallowed both and sank back onto my bed. Feeling lonely and frightened, I drifted fitfully off to sleep. The next couple of days were a complete write-off as far as I was concerned. Syd and the other musicians poked their heads round the door, the musicians to see if I was still alive and Syd (God bless him) probably worrying more about his production. The only other person to visit me was one of the hotel staff who braved all my germs and viruses to bring me food and drink. I can remember drinking lots of water and taking 'zee pills' and then feeling much better on the third day. I actually made the afternoon recording session. One more day's work and then, thankfully, I was on my way home.

But my ordeal was not yet over. A few days later, Syd called me into Lansdowne Studios to record the guitar parts that I'd been too ill to play. Adrian Kerridge and the studio had generously 'stretched' the mix downtime to allow me to record all the guitar parts to twenty titles. It took about four hours of nonstop work and as I had still not fully recovered from the virus — my energy level at the end of the session was at an all-time low. I was never so glad as when that whole episode was over.

Home Life

In 1970 Judy and I moved our family into a bigger house about four miles further from London. Located in Cheam, Surrey, just off the Sutton Bypass, it also offered good schools, village shopping and a peaceful sanctuary from the hustle and bustle of London Town.

Or so I thought.

There were large playing fields at the back of the house and with their expanse of green grass and stands of tall trees they made an added attraction. A good way across the playing field was Henderson Hospital. Originally used to treat the wounded of World War II and other military altercations, the buildings were later used for the treatment of mixed patients with mental disorders. The local residents were assured there would be no violent patients and lights once again appeared in the Hospital windows. Certainly no violent patients but, and I have this on good medical assurance, that people with such disabilities are very prone to cohabit — If you know what I mean!

Well, one winter morning in 1970 when Jayne was six years old, she came running into the house to tell Judy and me that there were people being rude in the field out the back. I went upstairs to the back bedroom and sure enough, there was this man and woman copulating beside a hedgerow. Such was the couple's intense concentration on the job in hand that they were totally unaware of the freezing conditions. Indeed, there must have been a good layer of frost on the gentleman's bare derriere. Maybe the freezing cold had frozen his dick solid as they were going at it non-stop. Judy called the police and within a few minutes a police car screeched to halt outside our house.

'Where's the fornication taking place?' the officer said, a little too eagerly.

'Out the back,' I replied. 'You can see from the upstairs back bedroom window.'

'Let's go there,' the officer said removing his helmet, once again, a little too eagerly.

Staring with great interest out the window for some time at the chilled non-stop gyrations, the officer said, 'I'll have to report this to the authorities,' and reluctantly moved away from the window.

Before the hospital officials and a couple of police officers arrived at the scene, however, the couple had departed, frozen, and (I hope) satisfied.

A few years later the hospital caught fire and was destroyed. I viewed the start of the inferno from the same back bedroom window and called the local newspaper.

'Any dead bodies?' the reporter on duty inquired.

Being told that as far as I knew there weren't, he put the phone down on me.

Strange!

The previous owners of our house had warned us there were plans afoot for an Ambulance Sub Station on the playing fields, but had no idea when or where it was scheduled to be built. Neither did anyone at the Council.

'Sub Station? What's a Sub Station?' we asked.

'Oh, just somewhere to park the spare ambulance,' came the answer. 'A sort of medical overflow.'

Three years after we moved in, the Council builders started digging and laying out the groundwork for the sub station. Our neighbors became distraught. The building with its attendant lights, bells, revving engines and ambulance driver chat grew from the green pastures at the bottom of their garden.

It was now too late to do anything. The Council had Spoken. The Council had Acted. The Council had Built. Having wielded their might, the Council moved on to the next socially impacting scheme. The book was closed on the subject of Ambulance Sub Stations.

After many complaints to indifferent Council employees, the neighborhood managed to stop the bells, sirens, ambulance men's loud radios and other anti environmental atrocities. A muted and strained peace was established.

Peace continued until a few years later when word spread throughout the community that the Sutton Bowling Club was moving into the area. The Council had decided the land the Club now occupied in central Sutton was much too valuable for tossing bowls around on so, in their infinite wisdom, moved the Club to the bottom of our garden. What's wrong with that? I can hear you saying. Surely, only the most respectable people played bowls and most of them would be over sixty and incapable of annoying anybody. Such perfect behavior would have been true back in the 1950s or 1960s. However, television, in its constant search for new audiences, had elevated bowls to the status of football, tennis or horse shows, and with its new status came prize money. With prize money comes great competition and competition brings a younger player with the exuberance of the soccer game — and its crowd!

Peaceful Sunday mornings and afternoons became a fond and fading memory. The distant sound of a lawn mower being carried by a warm summer breeze was replaced by the constant and resounding click-clicking of the bowls as they were aimed and then gathered. The gentle snip of garden shears lasting but a few minutes was usurped by the constant variations of 'Oh, well done, Old Chap!' and 'Good bowl!' and 'Come on, team!' The quiet conversation over the garden fence with one's neighbor was continually interrupted by loud and echoing applause. Complaints fell on deaf ears. After all, the game of bowls was enjoyed by the upper echelon of the community who, dressed in the mandatory 'whites' and wearing special shoes, would find it impossible to be responsible for such disturbing behavior as our letters described.

'Come and join us — see what fun it is,' was the Club secretary's rejoinder.

'Try and have a peaceful moment in our gardens,' was our reply.

It dawned on me that these people had no idea how intrusive their behavior was and following our efforts to inform them, I came to realize how insensitive they all were. Give them some of their own medicine, I thought. Let them hear what a din they make whilst they compete and click and applaud. I decided my weapon was going to be the very noise they made. I set out to amplify and play back to these people the sounds they were making. In the big trees at the back end of my garden I placed a couple of old speakers and aimed them at the Bowling Green nearest our garden. This green seemed to be favored by the most exuberant players and would give me a good strong 'signal.' Being picked up by a strategically placed microphone, this signal was amplified and played back. Disappointingly, apart from a few glances in the direction of the trees, there was no reaction.

Delay the sound. That was the answer. Putting an old tape delay and echo machine into the circuit enabled me to play back the bowlers sounds a couple of seconds after they were made. Every 'Well done, old boy!' that came my way winged its way back to the originators at least four or five times in diminishing volume. I found, with gleeful revenge, that the processing of the bowlers' applause was particularly effective. It was so effective it resulted in complaints to the authorities about me causing a disturbance and 'putting the members off their game.' On advice, I decided to abandon my aural guerrilla tactics, and instead every day I was home, prayed for weeds in the bowling greens and heavy rain. If I was going to suffer, so were they!

Being England, the rain I got, but diligent groundsmen kept the weeds at bay.

All that's mentioned above was going on at the back of the house. In the front was another whole world. Across the street, about six houses down was the Downs Lawn Tennis Club. Somehow the sound of tennis balls being hit was not so intrusive. Maybe it was the distance but that particular sound had, at least to me, a soporific effect. There was also a clubhouse attached to the tennis courts that served as a convenient watering hole after driving back from London. With the car safely in its garage, I had just a few steps to walk — there and back. Naturally, being so close, Judy and I were regular visitors and, as a consequence, I got ensnared in Committees and the various functions that were held in the Club House. Not a bad thing, I suppose, on reflection, but as anybody knows, who has had a similar experience, involvement with any social establishment means work and time. The work I didn't mind but the time was a different matter. When I became Secretary of the place, which was a foolish move, I found myself getting up at five in the morning to type license extension applications and other similar administrative tasks before driving up to London. Instead of being thanked for my efforts, I was criticized. If any small item was overlooked, such as getting the grammar wrong in a letter that I had hastily written just before rushing up to London for a full day of recording, then snide comments would come from all sides. Ask those same people to do the work and you wouldn't see their heels for dust.

The Cruise

One of the perks that developed in the session musicians' working lives in the '60s and '70s was 'the Cruise.' Shipping lines such as P & O and Cunard would engage a 'celebrity group' as added entertainment for the passengers and as a filler for use in all entertainment areas of the ship to give the other acts a break. (I very quickly learned that it is a ship and not a boat. You cruise in a ship and fish from a boat.) Cruises were an easygoing working vacation. Playing for an hour on selected nights it could hardly be called 'work.' Musicians were able to take their families with them and were provided with very nice accommodation. On one three-week cruise I did with the Jock Cumming Band, I was able to take Judy, Kevin and Jayne. A cabin on 'C' Deck with all the attendant luxuries was yours for the princely sum of 150 pounds sterling. Not a bad deal!

Although Jock Cummings was the name featured on the ship's programming, it was Freddy Staff (a trumpet player) that was the arranger and chief counter-inner. The band included Jock on drums, Freddy on trumpet, myself on guitar was Tim Bell on bass, Max Harris on piano and Cliff Townsend on sax and clarinet. (Cliff was Pete Townsend's father, by the way.) We had some interesting moments with Cliff and his wife Betty and it was easy to see where Pete got his talent and extrovert characteristics. The music we played was very main stream, with a leaning toward Dixieland. I realized, when we were many miles out to sea, that a banjo would have fitted in very nicely and given some of the numbers an added colour.

Some nights we played for dancing, some nights for just entertaining and one night we had to perform for the crew. The Crews Lounge area was right at the bow of the ship and was consequently more susceptible to the ship's movements. Notwithstanding any movement, it was not the most pleasant place to be, being devoid of atmosphere and full of Goanese who didn't understand or like western music.

The night we performed in the crew's quarters — or should I say *tried* to perform — was the stormiest of the whole three weeks. The first indication that conditions were very quickly deteriorating was when all the music stands tipped over and deposited music across the steel deck. It was impossible even to stand up let alone play an instrument. Max was holding onto the piano with one hand and trying to play with the other. Fortunately the piano was bolted to the floor, making Max the only member of the band not trying to keep his balance. I wasn't sorry when the performance was canceled and we could all get back to more pleasant surroundings. Kevin and Jayne, being eleven and nine respectively, loved the stormy conditions. The ability to 'float' up the stairs like an astronaut in space when the great ship plunged downwards gave them endless hours of pleasure. Not so pleasurable was lying in bed listening to the creaking and groaning of the hull as it crashed its way through the enormous waves. We were told by a ship's officer the Canberra had sailed safely through worse storms than the one we were experiencing, but it was still comforting to hear the distant, low-pitched hum of the engines when the other noises stopped for a few seconds. The same officer told me the Canberra did eighteen feet to the gallon, which made my 1973 Buick Riviera seem like an economy vehicle.

With several hundred passengers and about the same amount of crew trapped on board for three weeks it was no wonder that the odd 'incident' occurred. Appearing in cabaret on the ship was Joan Regan who had had a series of hit records in the 1950s and was now working the circuit. One night Miss Regan was performing in the Pool Lounge and, being a particularly pleasant evening, the great window that separated the lounge from the pool had been lowered into the deck.

Scheduled to play at 11.00 p.m. on a small stage by the pool, we were hastily called by the cruise director to assemble and be ready to start playing at 10.30 p.m. Max had been taking a nap in his cabin when the call came so he dressed and dashed up to the pool area. His hurry was evident by bleary eyes and his pyjamas showing at the bottom of his dress trouser legs. There we were, assembled ready to play, with our songbird crooning her way through a selection of romantic and slow ballads. The overly enthusiastic and super-energetic cruise director saw the evening's entertainment grinding to a sleepy halt. He walked briskly up to Freddy and said, 'To hell with this. It's like a funeral. Play something happy, right now.'

Freddy looked bewildered. 'Joan's still singing,' he said. 'We can't start yet.'

Our cruise director had slightly overfilled his tanks with liquid energy and enthusiasm. 'I said *play. Now!*' he commanded.

With a resigned look at the rest of us, Freddy put his trumpet to his lips and blasted out an invigorating introduction to 'Dinah.'

We all agreed that it was totally wrong to have started to play, but the cruise director's word was final. Passengers started to drift out of the lounge to listen to us and we could see Joan storming off the stage in the lounge. At the end of our first set a tall, distinguished-looking man came up to the front of the stage and shouted at Freddy, 'You are an ignorant pig for interrupting Miss Reagan's performance.'

Freddy could hardly control his temper, but he did and we spent the entire break trying to calm him down. As we played the last set I noticed this same man hovering above us on one of the seating areas around the pool.

'I said you are an ignorant pig and you should be thrown off the ship,' he shouted.

Freddy was once more consumed with anger and once more we held him back. Putting his clarinet in his case, I heard Cliff whisper to Freddy, 'I wouldn't stand for that if I were you. I'd bloody get him.'

'You're right!' shouted Freddy and took off like a wild bull, scrambling over the railings to get at this angry passenger. The passenger fled, with Freddy hot on his heels. Two of the crew who were starting to clear the decks managed to hold Freddy back just as the passenger disappeared through a doorway. If it wasn't so serious, it could have been funny.

Almost immediately word came from the Captain for Freddy and Jock to report to his office the next morning. The Golden Rule of cruise ships is Never Attack a Passenger — no matter what the passenger has said or done. Freddy had broken this rule. We were allowed to finish the cruise but the Jock Cummings band would never again work on a ship at sea. No amount of protestation would change the Captain's mind. He had spoken and that was that. The other passengers had only heard the so called victim's side of what happened and Freddy was viewed with disdain by many. The cruise director, whose fault it was, never mentioned the incident nor would he even discuss it with us. Nevertheless, we had some good times and got to visit places in the Caribbean which we would never otherwise have had the opportunity to see.

Our band wasn't alone in having altercations. Other musicians and bands met a similar disciplinary fate. When I went to my second season at Butlins in 1958, the musicians were no longer allowed to stay on the camp. Too many 'infractions' of camp rules had been reported and we were forced to look for digs in the town. This, of course, made a large hole in the money we were earning and led to discontentment within the band members.

I've been fortunate that the incidents I have personally been involved with have managed to miss the headlines. Another case of musicians overdoing things was with the Charlie Watts Big Band. Charlie, famous as the drummer with the Rolling Stones, loved big band music. His ambition was to form a big band of his own and to play some concerts.

The money he made with the Stones enabled him to fulfill this ambition. He commissioned arrangements and got an eighteen-piece band together to make a CD. Resplendent with two drummers, percussion, five trumpets and all the trimmings, everything looked set for success. All was well at the beginning but the off stage antics of some of the musicians during the concerts in Europe led to Charlie calling it a day and disbanding. Charlie returned to playing drums with the Stones and driving a tractor on his farm.

He was a nice guy with a shattered dream.

Dance Bands

Denny Boyce had a sixteen-piece band that was resident on the Mecca circuit, as it was then known. Denny was a frustrated guitarist and would insist on playing when a Rock and Roll number was performed. His guitar was picked up, plugged in and flayed by Denny whilst he looked querulously at me for confirmation that all was OK. I had to look away most times because his tuning and sense of timing left much to be desired. Eric Ford, Denny's regular guitarist, and I swapped many 'Denny stories' over tea breaks when working together on sessions or at social occasions. I personally love the story about Frank Gillespie and Denny's week at a Mecca Ballroom in Glasgow.

Frank, amongst his other interests, had a propensity to hit the bottle. So much so that at times he was semi-incapable of playing. I have seen Frank stand up to play a solo (in this instance a filler waltz), and the alto sax had drifted away from his mouth. No sound was forthcoming. The other players, now aware of the lack of melody, turned to see what had happened. There was Frank, swaying, with the saxophone mouthpiece some inches from his mouth yet he was still blowing and fingering the sax as if the sound was coming out. The funny part to me was that the player next to Frank put his hand up to the sax, gently pushed it back into Frank's mouth and the melody continued once again as if nothing had happened, as sweet as ever. The guys returned to their respective conversations without further comment.

Denny, God bless him, usually found this kind of episode highly amusing. But there was no such humour in Glasgow, Scotland. Frank had gone beyond even Denny Boyce's generous guidelines and Denny had fired him half way through the first night. Frank was now without a job or money — and was many hundreds of miles from home. Denny would not relent and had hired a lead alto from Glasgow.

The next night, as the bandstand rotated, a bedraggled figure stood on the dance floor in front of the stage, his saxophone and clarinet clasped in his hands and begging for his job back. Still Denny did not soften and the band played on whilst Frank slunk away into the night. This charade occurred for the next four nights, each night Frank appearing more bedraggled, unshaven and unkempt yet still clutching his gleaming sax and clarinet. Denny's heart finally took over from his head and Frank was given some money to smarten up and was rehired. It transpired that Frank had been living and sleeping in a broom-and-cleaning supply closet for the past few days — not eating and, with no money, certainly not drinking.

Confusion and loneliness finally got the better of him and dear Frank, even with all his wonderful talents, actually lay down with his head in a gas oven and took his life a few years later whilst suffering from severe depression. It was a great loss to the musical community.

Going back to my working with Eric Winston a comical — at least it seems so now — episode stands out. Eric had a twitch which he covered up by various actions he had trained himself to do. Being new to the band his movements weren't that obvious, especially as I had other things to concentrate on, like reading the music! However, on the first broadcast with the band at Piccadilly 1, actually Number 221 (why the different number I never figured out), the band was a minute away from transmission, again a live broadcast, and I looked up at Eric sitting at his podium. Eric winked at me! What a nice fella, I thought — trying to make me feel at home. So I winked back. My wink was returned with a scowl. Unbeknownst to me this was one of Eric's more nervous twitches, apparently brought on by the red transmission light flickering. Roy Marsh later took me aside to explain and describe the many twitches of Mr Winston.

The Bond Connection

Years after the initial recording of the James Bond Theme, Monty Norman had sued *Mojo* magazine for uttering statements he didn't like, and later suing *The Sunday Times* for repeating some of passages from the article. To try and win their case, *The Times* tried to prove that Monty Norman was not quite the composer he was making himself out to be and therefore not in a position to sue the paper. *The Times* didn't actually say that Mr Norman *wasn't* the Bond theme composer, but by reprinting parts of the *Mojo* article there was a kind of implication. To further their cause, *The Times* called John Barry and me, as well as a number of other involved people as witnesses. I was thoroughly tired of the continuing squabbling that had been going on and in reply to *The Times'* legal representative's request for my attendance at the Old Bailey in London; I shot off the following reply:

Without prejudice

To: Alastair Brett   Your Ref: ST/NOR/97/AJB
*   Times Newspapers Ltd   London*
From: Vic Flick
*   Santa Monica, California*
Date: October 2nd 1998

Dear Mr. Brett,
Thank you for your fax, dated 2nd October.

I have no wish to be further involved with Monty Norman's litigious career on the now sordid subject of who wrote the James Bond Theme.

Certainly, I was directly involved with the concept and the many recordings of the Theme but do not wish to be questioned on the matter. I am led to understand that John

Barry has acknowledged that Monty Norman wrote the theme — although I am not privy to whatever negotiations may have led to that statement. If Mr Norman wants even more, then I suggest you tell him to go squeeze the nearest rock.

Yours faithfully

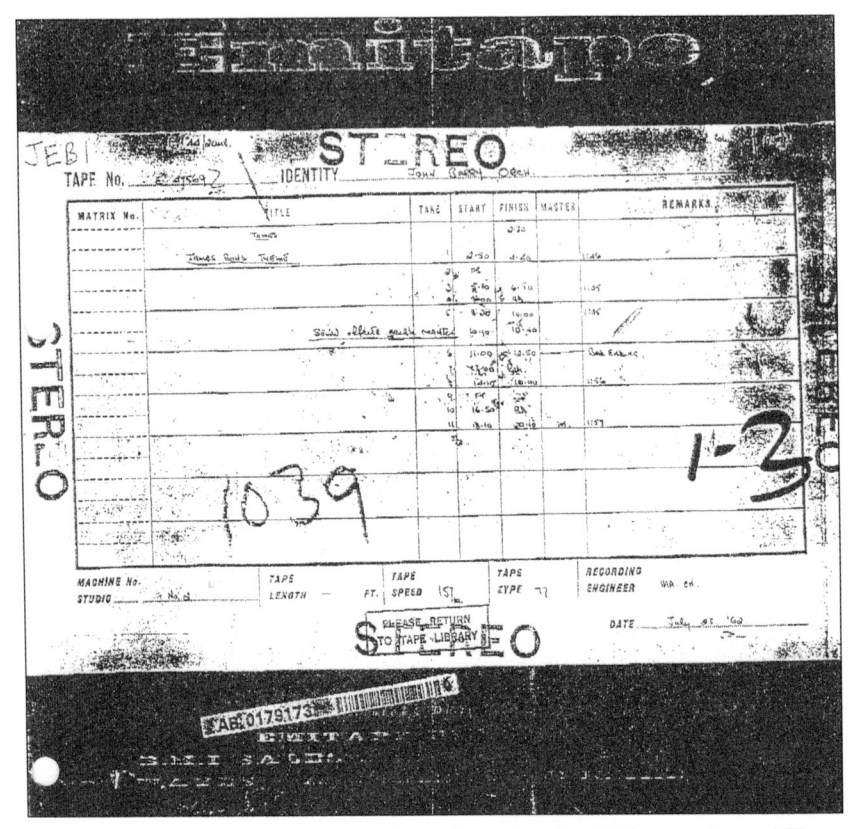

Above: Copy of the script on the Tape Case for the EMI recording of The James Bond Theme. 24 July, 1962.

Facing Page: Extracts from my diary showing 21 June and 24 July 1962, when the James Bond Theme was recorded for the film and again for the record.

Notwithstanding my reply, I was talked into going to London provided they hosted me in a fashion appropriate to the occasion. The Swiss Hotel located near the Law Courts, and in particular the Old Bailey, was a peaceful haven after the Business Class flight on British Airways from Los Angeles. I had signed a written deposition that was used in the proceedings, but a personal appearance was deemed necessary. So, in

THE BOND CONNECTION

JUNE, 1962

18 MONDAY (169—196)
Waterloo, 1815. ○ Full Moon

3 - 4 PHILLIPS ELEC.   6 | 10

19 TUESDAY (170—195)

7.30 - 10.30 olympia

20 WEDNESDAY (171—194)

7 30
34 Curzion 1

21 THURSDAY (172—193)
Corpus Christi. Longest Day

10 - 1   C.T.S.   ELEC + Acc. 2   5
2.30 - 5.30 PHILLIPS.   7 10
                ELEC
                        52 6

22 FRIDAY (173—192)
P.A.Y.E. Week 12 begins

2.30 - 5.30 PHILLIPS.
           ELEC.
8 - 11.45 LOCARNO.

23 SATURDAY (174—191)
s.r. 4.43, s.s. 9.21

BU STOL

24 SUNDAY (175—190)
1st after Trinity. S. John Baptist
Midsummer Day (Quarter Day)

4. oclock
BRISTOL

JULY, 1962

23 MONDAY (204—161)   S Mayor
                9 - 30 -
                10 30   6 18
10.30 - 12.30   E.M.I

24 TUESDAY (205—160)
☾ Last Quarter

2.30 - 4.30 E.M.I.
     J Barry
           06 6

25 WEDNESDAY (206—159)
S. James

26 THURSDAY (207—158)

27 FRIDAY (208—157)
P.A.Y.E. Week 17 begins

DUNSTABLE

28 SATURDAY (209—156)
s.r. 5.17, s.s. 8.55

CARDIFF
SOPHIA GARDEN

29 SUNDAY (210—155)
6th after Trinity

March 2001, armed with this statement and copies of the relevant pages from my 1962 diary, I fought my way through the inclement weather up the hill from The Swiss Hotel by the Thames and into the Old Bailey. It was an imposing building, the interior of which was full of many serious-looking people rushing about with mountains of paper and folders. Surprisingly small and musty, the court where the trial was taking place was in direct contrast to the vastness of the building.

After waiting for a couple of days my moment finally arrived. My name was called and I proceeded with some trepidation to the witness box. The legal body for *The Times* had advised me in most somber terms only to answer the questions and not to elaborate. With this caveat in mind, I faced the Defense Attorney's questions and the twelve 'good men and true' in the jury seated across the Court Room. Following simple answers to what I considered simple questions, I then expected to face a grilling from the Prosecution. To my relief (and in some measure my disappointment), the Prosecution had no questions and I was asked to step down. *The Times'* legal representative took me angrily to one side and demanded to know why I hadn't explained this point or elaborated. I told him I was following his orders. With a legal-sounding grunt, he turned away and that was the end of my Old Bailey experience. Following days of procedures, lengthened by John Barry being indisposed, the trial resulted in *The Times* losing, Monty Norman getting $50,000 plus expenses and, hopefully the matter being put to rest.

Mr Norman has jealously guarded his composition for many years. He insisted that there should always be a credit on every film stating the Theme was his. He even had his attorney send me a letter so that I would verify John Barry had stated in public Mr Norman wrote the Theme. The litigation on this matter seemed unending. I can understand his paranoia. Mr Norman has lived very comfortably off that single tune for the major part of his life.

It was now legally documented that Monty Norman wrote The 'James Bond Theme.' He won his case and is now legally proven to be a composer of good standing and, without doubt, the composer.

Being directly involved with the piece of music, I was always under the impression that Mr Norman's writings were turned into something commercial by John Barry to which I added the guitar sound and the interpretation. Together we made the recordings successful and distinctive. Mr Norman has made many hundreds of thousands of pounds. John Barry has made millions from the spin off. I made about seven pounds ten shillings — and he should send *me* a letter from his attorney? I ought to have made considerably more than I did if the Musicians' Union had their act together back in the 1960s.

I did occasionally benefit peripherally from the films and the record.

Many musical directors booked me for 'the sound' and to recreate the other guitar passages in the score. In the latter part of the 1970s, Roland Shaw was making some covers of James Bond music for the Readers Digest and I received a call from Sid Sax, Roland's fixer.

'Did you do the guitar solo for the Gypsy encampment scene in *From Russia with Love*?' he asked.

Confirming that I did, he booked me for a session at Decca Studio 3.

'You will get a solo fee added to the basic,' Sid assured me and a few days later I dutifully turned up at the studio. On the guitar part placed on my music stand, where the solo was to be, there appeared a few bars with nothing in them apart from 'Solo Ad Lib' written over the top. At least there were a few bar lines giving an approximate length and not just the single bar with a pause mark over it as on John Barry's original score.

'You can remember what you played,' Roland said, smiling, as he gave the down beat to the massive orchestra.

Remember what I played? It was years ago! I put the brain and fingers on automatic pilot and came up with a satisfactory rendition of the original. Sid smiled a 'well done' and pressed the usual little brown envelope into my hand at the end of the session. Just before getting in my car to go to the next date, I opened the envelope.

One pound extra! Can you believe that?

The guitar I used on the film sessions for the Theme and on the early recordings was a Clifford Essex Paragon with a DeArmond Pick Up gripped by its supporting plates to the strings behind the bridge, and held away from the body of the guitar by a carefully folded Senior Service Cigarette Packet. There is a story going about that the guitar I used was a cracked old guitar that was so useless that it had to be thrown away after the session — and that's why the 'sound' could never be created again. Peter Hunt, the editor on many Bond films is alleged to have made that statement.

I can assure the reader the guitar is in very good condition and, as of this writing, languishing in The Rock and Roll Hall of Fame in Cleveland, Ohio.

The selection of strings available in the late 50s and early 60s was abysmal compared to today. I think it used Cathedral wire wound with a .058" low 'E' and a .012" top 'E' plucked with a tortoise shell plectrum. To get that 'overplayed sound,' I simply overplayed the guitar, leaning into those thick low strings with the very hard plectrum. Jennings Music in Charing Cross Road had given the Seven some Vox Amplifiers for publicity purposes and I used one of the Vox 15s. The film track was recorded at the CTS Studios in Bayswater, a studio where so many famous film sound tracks were recorded.

The Bond theme studio set up was for an orchestra and not a Pop session, so many of the aural characteristics we are used to today are missing. Some of my guitar sound was picked up on the many open microphones placed about the studio for the other musicians. This gave a 'room' effect that added to the general ambiance. In no way was it as bad as the earlier experience at Denham, but it was the 'orchestral' way of doing things and John Barry and the recording engineer (the one and only Eric Tomlinson) wanted the orchestral sound coupled with the punch of the guitar and the brass. It worked. Even today that sound is so distinctive it holds its own. We recorded the theme for the film at CTS and also recorded it again at EMI, managing to nearly capture the same feel and sound. In fact the arrangement was recorded several times for inclusion in promotions and for dropping into soundtracks of later Bond movies.

In 1989, when Michael Kamen was recording the music track for the Bond film, *License to Kill*, another of my 'nearly made it' episodes occurred. One day I received a call from Michael's contractor (again, Sid Sax) checking to see if I would be available to 'do' a couple of days at a studio on the Goldhawk Road near Shepherds Bush. I was available, and wrote the details in my diary. Sid was never too descriptive of what you were booked for. Once a musician was established in Sid's book there were three criteria he operated by:

You were alive

You could do the date

You couldn't do the date.

Sid did give me the 'phone number of the recording engineer. Apart from this break in protocol I soon learned that the booking was a little different.

Arriving at the studio and entering the control room, I was surprised to see Eric Clapton sitting on a chair and working out a riff on his guitar. I hadn't seen Eric for a long time — not since some of those New Musical Express concerts way back in the 1960s when he was playing with one of the groups he was associated with. Eric and I chatted about those times whilst the studio was being set up. Eric is a totally pleasant man who I am proud to know.

I was introduced to Michael Kamen and the story started to unfold. Michael and Eric had been commissioned to compose and record the theme for the next Bond movie, *License to Kill*. Michael wanted to get back to the original sound for a low bass type riff and it was hoped that I could furnish it. The melody and other parts were to be laid on top of my low guitar riff. I had the same guitar, the same foot pedal, and I think, the same guitar cord, but I didn't have the old Vox amp. The

THE BOND CONNECTION 127

On the *License to Kill* set

original amp had fallen off a stage many years ago and the speaker cone had torn and the casing splintered. This Vox amp could have been the key to the sound, but try as we may, we couldn't emulate the original. I'd brought along a Peterson Amplifier, a versatile amp that tried as hard as it could to give us what we were looking for. All day we worked on this composition and by the close it was sounding pretty good. I was in the process of packing up my gear when I was approached by what can only truthfully be described as the 'suits.'

A very quick meeting was held in which everything was explained to me. The recording that I had just taken part in was to be the theme for the next Bond movie. The recording and the next day's videoing ('videoing?') was to be used as the world-wide publicity of the Bond movie. The video was to be used as the new world-wide Advertising Campaign for Coca-Cola and would be used on MTV to promote the single that was soon to be released. It appeared that the main reason the 'suits' had flown in from New York was to talk about signing me up to a mega-buck record deal. CD titles were falling from their lips like water over Niagara Falls...

'Vic Flick plays the Mighty Bond Themes'
'Vic Flick plays the Great Guitar Hits'
'The Romantic Guitar of Vic Flick'
And so on and so on...

The amazing thing was that these guys were so serious about everything. What they said, they believed, as if their jobs depended on it — which was probably true.

This was my moment! At last, I was going to be a STAR!

That evening I actually called John Barry to see if the whole thing was a set up and, if it wasn't, what was I to do?

'Don't sign any papers, and if you're in doubt about anything, check with Don Black,' was John's advice.

Check with Don Black! Wow! Was I in the big league or was I in the big league?

The next morning a limo arrived to take me to the London Dock area. The day was to be spent in the attic of a riverside wharf making a video of us all completing the recording we had started the previous day. Ray Cooper (Elton John's celebrated bongo player) was there, as were some other shining stars of the Pop World whose names escape me, including an American drummer specially imported for the sessions. The day sped by with plenty of action, plenty of food and, at the end, plenty of all-round congratulations for a job well done.

I left the location with a sense of hope that maybe, and I emphasize the word '*maybe*,' something was going to happen. Days dragged by with no word from anybody, let alone the 'suits.' In desperation, I called

Michael Kamen to find out what was happening on the 'star' front.

'Oh,' he said, in answer to my question. 'We're very disappointed. Michael Edwards and the production team didn't like the instrumental and it has now been rejected.'

You're disappointed, I thought to myself.

'They didn't like the track at all,' he continued. 'Wasn't what they were looking for. Gladys Knight and the Pips are doing the theme song now. I'll see you on the music sessions.'

I didn't hear another word from anybody about those couple of days — or even get to see the video. That's Show Biz for you! The completed video and sound recording have been sought by James Bond aficionados ever since.

There have been many James Bond films and many composers. John Barry's scores were the definitive Bond music and David Arnold has done a magnificent job of creating the same atmosphere with his scores. Sir George Martin, Michael Kamen, Marvin Hamlisch and Bill Conti all left their mark on the Bond dynasty. *License To Kill,* with music by Michael Kamen, was the last Bond film I worked on.

As every body seems to agree, Sean Connery was THE James Bond. He had that ruggedness and charm that was the very epitome of a spy. George Lazenby kinda blew it and was soon followed by Timothy Dalton. Timothy was a good actor and a very affable guy. We had a few beers together with the other musicians in the bar at the New CTS in Wembley. After Roger Moore, who brought a touch of *The Saint* Television series with him to the Bond films came Pierce Brosnan who brought a new dimension to the starring role.

Jumping forward in time to 2005, Judy, my son Kevin and I were in 'Chiatzis on Main' in Santa Monica, a bar and restaurant made famous by being partly owned by Arnold Schwarzenegger. Suddenly, we spotted Pierce Brosnan standing at the other end of the bar. Judy, being Judy, went up to Pierce and told him of my connection to the Bond films. He insisted in walking around the bar to meet me and talk about the films. Many questioning eyes were on him as he approached, and those eyes must have widened with curiosity when he stopped to talk at length with me. We enjoyed swapping tales of our very different involvements with the Bond films until his wife arrived and reminded him of an appointment. A true gentleman with fine principles and a dedicated film maker.

The Beatles Connection

EMI, or Abbey Road Studios as it is now called, was always busy. When the Beatles were in their prime, about 1964 and onwards, John, Paul, Ringo and George could often be seen in Number 2 studio working out a song or just laying about. We might be in Studio 3 knocking out four or five titles in three hours whilst the 'Lads from the 'Pool' would take a whole day to decide what the title would be. Such a luxury in those days when, 'get as many titles recorded in as little time as possible for as little money as possible,' was the rule.

Working at EMI as much as I did, there were many times I would see and chat with members of the Beatles who would be in the canteen taking a break for a 'cuppa' or just enjoying the change of environment. They were all good guys. I enjoyed John Lennon's dry humour and admired his songwriting abilities. To me, he was the driving force of the Beatles and his presence is sorely missed to this day. John, Paul, George and Ringo made great contributions to the world of Pop music with their energy, harmonies and innovative style. I don't think they were aware of their future influence when they were recording their songs, any more than any musician or artist at that time could have envisioned how long their recordings would last. Maybe with architects, engineers, and authors aside, who else other than recording musicians would be made constantly aware of work they had done forty or fifty years ago?

In the words of journalist Matt Hurwitz, in 1977, EMI released what has become Paul McCartney's most obscure and least known album of his career — *Thrillington*. The album, an instrumental, orchestrated version of his *Ram* LP, was hardly noticed by the press or the rest of the music world. Hardly surprising, considering the almost complete absence of Paul's name anywhere on the album. Even the artist was listed as someone else — somebody named Percy "Thrills" Thrillington.

A wonderful and innovative arranger and composer, Richard Hewson, planned out a neat breakup of the arrangements for the album in order to economically record all of the material in the three days allotted. Unlike a rock recording (a Beatles one, for example), where musical ideas are often worked out in the studio, orchestrated arrangements already have the ideas planned out — on paper, no less. All titles featuring strings, for instance, can have the strings recorded in one morning session, and those requiring horns can have them added in a later evening session.

The first session took place on Tuesday, June 15th at 10 a.m. in Studio Two ("the downstairs one, where all the Beatle recordings took place," says Hewson). The "basic tracks" for all tunes on the album consisted of a "pop combo," onto whose recordings the other instruments would be added as overdubs. The pop combo was recorded in this morning session. The group included veteran session guitarist Vic Flick and popular session drummer Clem Cattini, whose group the Telstars had had a big hit in the UK in 1962 with "The Tornados."

The bassist in the group was Herbie Flowers, who, besides recording with Lou Reed and numerous others, would, nearly ten years later, record with George Harrison and Ringo Starr. The piano was played by Steve Grey, who later would join Herbie Flowers's own group, Sky (those later albums, by the way, would be co-produced and engineered by Tony Clark). The organ was played by Roger Coulan, and percussionist Jim Lawless rounded out the group.

Flowers recalls, "We were all favorite musicians of Paul's." Flowers, in fact, later appeared on McCartney's *Give My Regards to Broad Street,* as well as on recordings by his brother Mike and his group, Scaffold. The musician's skill is evident throughout the record, particularly in the wide variety of basses heard throughout the album. "We read from sheet music. There was no improvising; we just played what was there." Had he heard the *Ram* album before the session? "We were all working 12 or 14 hour days. We rarely had time to listen to any albums. If I did," notes Flowers, a jazz fan, "I listened to Charlie Parker!" (Flowers currently can be heard in the South of England with his new jazz trio, Thompson's Directory.)

Wandering about 'supervising' the Beatles was George Martin. The Fab Four's music certainly needed a little smoothing round the edges and George Martin did a good job of that. Martin was just lucky that Dick Rowe turned the group down and gave him his chance. I did hear that Martin didn't want to record the Beatles at all but did so to secure his position at EMI. But that's only a rumour. With his aristocratic air and classical training, maybe Mr Martin had his eyes set on loftier projects. Whatever the case, with the Beatles outstanding success he definitely came up smelling of roses and, Boy, did he exploit it. Suddenly he was 'Mr Know-It-All of the Recording Business.'

Around the time when his success was set in concrete, a controversy was raging over Pop groups using session musicians to make their records. The groups would then go on television and mime to the recording. For some reason that now escapes me, this was thought to be a cardinal sin. One morning, driving to work, I heard Mr Martin — he with the flowing hair — being interviewed on the radio. I couldn't believe my ears. George Martin was saying, 'I don't agree with session musicians playing on Pop groups' records. After all, The Beatles, when they're in the studio with me, always play on their own records. Session musicians are unimaginative robot-like people who can only play what you tell them to. I only use them when I have to.'

He continued in a similar vein for another few minutes forgetting, of course, how he had used that wonderful drummer Andy White on drums for Beatles recordings plus many other 'robots' needed to dress up their work.

Getting to whichever studio it was that morning, I found quite a few of my colleagues had heard the broadcast. Martin was definitely not the flavor of the month. Just a few days later, I arrived at EMI and found that the session was, lo and behold, for Mr Golden Baton himself. A small rhythm section had been booked to record a basic backing track for some EMI contract artist. Drum parts were usually written like I////I////I////I etc. and within a few bars the drummer would get some idea of what was needed. Guitar parts, and sometimes bass parts, were similar except for chord notation as in: IDm7///IG9///IC///I etc.

Again, it's all too often left to the player to figure out what was wanted.

With Martin's broadcast in mind, we all quickly decided to play the parts as written, which weren't too dissimilar to those described above. Of course, the music sounded plodding and lifeless. We kept it going till waved to a halt by a reddening George Martin.

'I understand what's happening,' he said. 'You heard the broadcast. 'Well, the interview was taken out of context [which it wasn't] and I didn't mean what it sounded like [which he did].'

Following this effort at an apology, our professionalism took over and we managed to make something of the arrangement. We didn't hear any more interviews with him on that subject, I'm pleased to say, and after a while the debate over Pop groups using session musicians died down. I recorded a lot of music with Sir George and apart from that one incident our relationship was professional and very cordial.

Whatever momentary professional *faux pas* George may have made that had upset the world of the recording musician, he was very good at his job, arranging and composing some good music. He wrote the score for one of the Bond movies, *Live and Let Die*, in 1973. I suppose his connection with Linda and Paul McCartney, who penned the title song, helped him get the job. His score ranks up there with one of the best. His connection with The Beatles secured his 1964 involvement with *A Hard Day's Night*, the definitive Rock and Roll comedy film.

In a recent interview, Sir George talked of his scoring of the instrumental version of 'This Boy.' Retitled 'Ringo's Theme,' and used in the film as background to Ringo's walkabout, he wanted to get a distinctive sound for the heavily featured solo guitar. In his recorded interview, Sir George says he wanted a similar sound to the 'James Bond Theme' guitar and had booked me for the sessions. Not as strident or percussive as the

1962 Fender Vibrolux Amplifier. This Amplifier was used almost continuously throughout the 1960s and early 1970s. Well used, well worn with a great sound. Also pictured is an original 'Gibson Maestro Fuzz Tone' (circa 1965)

Bond theme, the sound I got nevertheless complemented the arrangement. The Clifford Essex guitar I used for the Bond theme had been put out to pasture, except for the occasional big band recording, so I used my 1962 Fender Stratocaster with a 1962 Fender Vibrolux amplifier to try and get a similar sound. George Martin was happy with the result and so was I, again, never dreaming that I would still be hearing the recording in the 21st Century.

Many years later I played at the House of Blues on Sunset Boulevard in Los Angeles with the Fab Four, an American Beatles sound and look-alike group — and very good they were, too. I hadn't realized the impact the tune had on people or the memories the tune evoked. As I started to play it, I noticed the crowd had stopped dancing and were standing on the dance floor, some right in front of the stage. And then, amazingly, I noticed men and boys, women and girls with tears in their eyes, arms

THE BEATLES CONNECTION

Vic at the House of Blues, Sunset Blvd., Los Angeles, 2004

around each other, swaying to the music. Leaving the stage area I was greeted by many of the audience and thanked for my performance. It was a very emotional and special moment. I did some other work with the Martin/Beatles combination but 'Ringo's Theme' was the title that put my guitar in the forefront.

Among the Girls

I have the happiest memories of recording, concert or TV appearances with so many lovely ladies, some as professional as could be, others absolute newcomers who obviously had that special 'something.' There were very few of the hit makers who had absolutely nothing at all going for them. Let's face it: even Cilla Black had good songs, as well as a friendly personality. She was a charmer to work for, a nice girl, but I just couldn't stand her voice. I was on half a dozen or more of her hits, from 'Anyone who had a Heart' early in 1964 right through to 'Something Tells Me' in '71, and I never could see what The Beatles had seen in her musically to whisk her to stardom from the cloakroom of the Cavern. When people in the music business outside Liverpool saw her for the first time, it was that classic case of us all looking at one another with that 'what the hell's going on here?' look in our eyes. She didn't look like much, so we thought she must have had a great voice.

Wrong!

Please let me say that I think Cilla is a star with all the bells and whistles such an adjective involves. Cilla has been taken to the hearts of the British people and deserves every accolade.

Shirley Bassey had some very good songs indeed, and everything that was needed to put them over. Oh, but I did find her difficult to work with! She always had something to say about how the song should go, but never seemed to think it was the right time for her to sing. Miss Bassey recorded that wonderful Bond song, 'Goldfinger,' in 1964. So emotional did she get during the recording that in the effort to reach the high sustained note at the end, she pulled off her bra and flung it over the vocal booth. As the orchestra watched this display, I expect all the musicians would have volunteered to do another take, perhaps in a higher key!

Miss Bassey did a tour of the UK with the John Barry Orchestra backing her. I worked the tour and, like the other musicians, wondered why there was always a day or days between concerts. The abundance of time off meant long drives back and forth to London from many towns 'up north.' A clue as to why such arrangements had been made was John Barry never being available between the concert dates and Miss Bassey and John always appeared together at the next venue—a coincidence perhaps? But to get to that glorious point, with all the rehearsals and false starts, it was always such a hassle, with little or no thanks for your efforts.

There were always fun and games when working with Dorothy Squires. She was forever in battle with the world around her, fighting some perceived injustice or other. 'Plucky Dot,' the press called her, though they'd probably use the word 'feisty' today. Just as Frank Sinatra was always 'Mr Francis Albert Sinatra, Old Blue Eyes Himself', and 'Stardust' was never just 'Stardust' but 'Hoagy Carmichael's "Stardust"' (a presenter's habit that paid scant regard to Johnny Mercer, who wrote the words), Dorothy Squires was eternally plucky.

Her talk was muckier. She had a mouth on her like a fishwife and her musical director had a penchant for libation. In fact he was the only person I know who was arrested for being drunk in charge of a pram. Apparently, his wife was away and left him to look after the baby. He parked the pram outside a pub for about five hours before coming out to find the poor little kid screaming and the police on the scene. The charge was 'drunk in charge of child,' in fact, but we always liked to think of it as 'drunk in charge of a pram.' With a few drinks to give him some Dutch courage, he'd have steaming rows with Dorothy Squires in the studio, completely oblivious to the studio full of musicians

'How do you expect me to sing that fucking note?' she'd shout form the vocal booth.

'Just sing the damn thing,' he'd reply, getting redder and redder in the face.

'Bastard!' she'd hiss.

'Cow!' he'd snarl.

If there are any out-takes around, they must be a blast.

It's easy to think of Dorothy Squires as a 'silly old moo' who by the end of her life was so down on her luck that she relied on the charity of a long-time admirer and of Roger Moore, who married her early in his career. Her enthusiasm for her husband, in fact, was a big factor in him becoming a film actor and—eventually—the third James Bond. Dorothy was a big star in the early 'fifties, and even by the time I was working with her she was still getting records in the charts. 'For Once in My Life' for eleven weeks late in 1969, 'Till' — jokingly known as the cash register song or the 'Jewish National Anthem' — for another eleven weeks in the spring of 1970, and 'My Way' for 23 weeks in the second half of that year. The fact that 'My Way' was around at the peak of her little Indian summer of success was one of life's lucky breaks for her, because no one could sing the song with more credibility. There's even a myth around that Dorothy Squires' version of 'My Way' sold more in Britain than Sinatra's. This is nonsense, but it shows the kind of aura around her, people's feeling that there was more to her than met the eye.

No agent or theatre group would book her for concerts so Dorothy would hire theatres, pay for the hall, the band, everything, and sell her own tickets. So loyal were her fans that every show would be sold out. No matter the audience was comprised of the same people. Every night was like a reunion with the bars and foyer crowded. It was difficult to hear the bell sounding the start of the concert for all the loud conversation and clinking of glasses. But every concert was successful; it fed her ego and made a lot of people very happy.

I was never one of Dusty Springfield's main men in the recording studios, though I was on her first solo hit, 'I Only want to be with You,' at Philips late in 1963, and on 'In the Middle of Nowhere' a couple of years later. I had a lot of respect for what she did — in that I thought she was a great Pop singer — but I could hardly recognise the woman I'd worked with when I read her obituaries in 1999.

'White soul diva?' I don't think any of us thought of her as that.

On one of the concert tours I did with John Barry, I accompanied her when she was one of the Lana Sisters—this is back in 1960. I did a couple of rhythm arrangements for them and we were always pleasant to each other. There had been more of a Country feel to her early work with the Lana Sisters, and especially the Springfields — and when it came to turning out her own hits, which she did with great success right through to the end of the sixties, she seemed too versatile to be put into any one particular bag.

In truth, Dusty Springfield wasn't a great mixer with studio musicians — we all knew she had her own agenda in life — but she could be awkward at times. I remember when she was working with Buddy Rich, the American drummer and bandleader who had a vicious mouth on him. As an aside, Buddy's guys once wound him up on the band bus, and the resulting covert recording is one of the funniest things I've ever heard. Anyway, Dusty started giving Buddy a hard time at rehearsals for a show, but unusually for him, he just didn't rise to the bait, and his musicians just couldn't understand it at all. He didn't even react when, come the end of rehearsals, she wanted it all done again, different tempos and everything. What he was doing, in fact, was saving his revenge for the show, when after a few introductory numbers by his orchestra he walked up to the microphone and said, without emotion: 'Ladies and gentlemen, the band singer.'

Dusty stalked on with a face like thunder, but, like a professional, she still gave the audience their money's worth.

Nancy Sinatra came to London to record some tracks for her *Nancy in London* album. Being part of the Sinatra enclave, she was accompanied by the usual group of hangers-on. English musical director, Johnny Harris, who had taken up residence in the USA, was the arranger, and the producer was a little guy who looked like he'd just come out of the jungle in Vietnam. Indeed, John wore the military paraphernalia any Navy Seal would be proud of, and that was just to conduct an orchestra. Completely immersed in the American studio jargon, John would regale us with quarters and measures instead of crotchets and bars.

A similar incident happened with Sammy Davis, Jr. With Johnny Harris again we were in the New Olympic and from the presence of the reporters and photographers we knew something was about to happen. Sure enough, in true 'American Star' tradition, Sammy swept into the studio surrounded by a strong arm entourage who huddled round the podium with Johnny. After much discussion, 'showbiz' laughter and gesticulations, the huddle crabbed its way to the singer's booth for the recording to start. As usual we never knew what was going on, but I think the song was for a film. The song was good, the band was great and Sammy was wonderful — full of energy and talent. Once the take was OK'd, the huddle gathered itself and funneled its way out the studio door never to be seen again. I tell friends I've worked with Sammy Davis, Jr. and they ask, 'did you talk with him?'

Talk with him? I was lucky to see the top of his head!

On a lighter note, there's a TV show that comes to mind when, with an orchestra conducted by Bob Leper. We were sentenced to accompany a singer from America by the name of Mrs Miller. The music seemed quite normal for the type of singer she appeared to be. A couple of standards, a couple of semi-operatic things and some light music. Big Jim and I were seated on a small stage about six feet from each other, with Jim slightly behind me. We had rehearsed all the music, checked the proliferation of wrong notes and were finally introduced to Mrs Miller. A middle-aged housewife type of person with severe delusions of grandeur, she was continually being circumnavigated by her simpering, petulant manager. He literally got in everybody's way. She thought he was needed so he stayed. Mrs Miller was very ordinary in every way until she opened her mouth and sung. Bob Leper had warned us that the lady was different and that she took her singing very seriously. With only just a few measures under her belt we became aware of how different she was and how sadly serious she was.

Mrs Miller was dreadful. No other word springs to mind that could adequately describe her. Her timing was dreadful. Her intonation was dreadful. Her whole approach to music itself was dreadful.

I had noticed that the audience seating area in the studio was filled to capacity — and that was just with studio personnel. The word was out. This was a 'special.' The first number began innocently enough with everyone managing to keep a straight face. Big Jim, however, when he decided something was funny, had to laugh. And nothing could stop him. Out of the corner of my eye I could see Jim's shoulders starting to shake and, looking at him over my shoulder, his face starting to turn a bright red. By comparison, Bob Leper's pale face took on a pleading expression as he foresaw what was going to happen. To make matters worse, we could see the audience trying, unsuccessfully, to contain their laughter. This in its turn made it harder for us to keep a straight face. When Mrs Miller, with her head back and hands clasped together, went for a particular high note and missed it by a mile the whole studio erupted into shrieks of laughter that any comedian could have built his career on. To compound this hysterical moment, Mrs Miller's manager rushed onto the set. The whole scene was too much. Bob Leper lowered his baton in resignation and the orchestra ground to a stumbling, blubbering halt. Jumping up and down and waving his arms, the manager demanded that everybody not connected with his artiste leave the studio. This type of order should only come from the producer but, as we later learned, he had been rendered incapable of coherent speech. When we started up again the hysteria had gone and a kind of sympathetic sadness had set in.

The story behind this tragicomedy is this. The poor lady's husband had passed away a couple of years before and left her a great deal of money. Firmly convinced she could sing, and without her husband to hold her back, she hired herself a manager and made an album. As is the way of these things, the album had become a big novelty hit in the States and no drunken party worth its salt would be held without a copy on the turntable. (This was before CDs!) The good lady actually hired the Carnegie Hall in New York. The hall was packed to capacity with 'fans.' Believing the public loved her for her voice she had set out to conquer the world.

Nobody has ever heard of her again. But as a memory, she will last forever.

A lovely lady to work with was Alma Cogan, perhaps not known internationally, but a good singer. Chris Curtis, drummer with the hit Pop group 'The Searchers' turned to producing records and one of his artists was Alma. Here's a quote from an interview Chris had with a music magazine about a recording in 1965:

> Interviewer: *You also made a single with Alma Cogan.*
>
> CC: *Yes, she was lovely, just the nicest person in the whole wide world. She was very up on the groups, she loved John Lennon and her best friend was the manager of the Ad-Lib in Leicester Square, which is where the bands used to meet. I wrote 'Snakes And Snails' for her and she was made up with it. I got Bobby Ore on drums, John Paul Jones on bass, Jimmy Page, Vic Flick and Joe Moretti on guitars and they played out of their skins. She didn't realise that she'd have to sing over a heavy rock backing and she loved it. The backing vocalists were Dusty Springfield, Doris Troy, Rosetta Hightower from the Orlons, and me. Boy, did we have fun.*

John Barry's ex-wife Jane Birkin went off with the Frenchman Serge Gainesboro. He looked weird and wild with his blue chin, but I liked the guy, and she obviously thought the world of him. When I say I played on their record *'Je T'Aime... Moi Non Plus'* in the summer of sixty-eight, you probably think I've got a tale or two to tell about it. 'Fraid not. It was as seemly and decorous as a Winifred Atwell session, and all those 'ooohs' and 'aaahs' and heavy breathings that had it banned from the air and made it a hit were clearly put on long after we'd left. (Now that session really would have been fun!)

In the bit involving me, Roger Coulham tootled away on the organ, while my backing was just about as 'routine' as could be. Peter Olaf was recording engineer at Philips, and I suspect he reveled in his contribution to the record, piecing together all the strands with technology that would seem very primitive today.

With Françoise Hardy it was the other way around. We expected cool sophistication and she turned out to be a right little raver. Her image in France was intellectual and existentialistic. We never got to know much about her intellect down at the PYE studio, but if one aspect of Existentialism is living for the moment, then I suppose we should have been more prepared for what happened.

She didn't strike me as pretty. I thought she had a long face with warts on it, and her hair was all over the place, though many guys raved about her and called her Françoise 'Ardon. She came along with her boyfriend, a drip in glasses as I recall, and they were literally all over each other — hands up skirts and down trousers — as we were trying to rehearse. It was early in 1965, and the songs we were recording included, *'Le Temps Des Souvenirs,'* part of her album unimaginatively called 'Francoise Hardy.' It was a pretty and wistful little album, but the action on those chairs beneath the big control room windows at PYE told a very different story.

Petula Clark was also on a Gallic kick when I was recording with her, helping her build a fabulously successful 'sixties career after everyone had written her off as a 'fifties pre-rock balladeer. I was on 'Downtown' in 1964 and a few other discs of hers, and I must say I liked her and thought she looked great. So did the teenagers of the time, and it was through Pet Clark that a lot of guys in their late teens discovered for the first time that it was possible to fancy somebody over the age of eighteen.

The 'French thing' of hers I was talking about stemmed from her marrying Claude Wolff, publicity man for the Paris-based Vogue record label, in 1959. They lived in the South of France in great luxury, and one of its spin-offs was that Pet took to wearing very little clothing. In fact, she admitted to walking around at home with nothing on at all and recommended other women to do the same, a piece of advice that didn't go down well with housewives living in terrace houses in Wolverhampton or Darlington or New Hope, PA. She didn't quite carry the doctrine into the recording studio, but she was still on a great *au naturelle* kick, with no bra, loose clothes, perhaps just a shirt tied at the bottom and a diaphanous skirt. I found it a bit embarrassing, to tell the truth. It was all a long way from the time she was best known in showbiz as Joe 'Mr Piano' Henderson's long-time date, an arrangement that was apparently the despair of her parents. Tony Hatch arranged and wrote her numbers, and between the two of them they were good sessions. She'd have Ronnie Price on piano, Ronnie Verrell on drums, Bryan Daly, I think — and me.

Sandie Shaw was a good kid but was emotionally insecure, then; professionally insecure, too, since she never did think she could sing. She wasn't exactly Dame Nellie Melba, it was true, but she had nothing to worry about. People liked her, they liked her songs, they liked Ken Woodman's arrangements and they loved the bare feet — a gimmick dreamed up by Eve Taylor, who had signed her up after being introduced to her by Adam Faith. I worked in Philips with her, and always had a high regard for Woodman, who was very much in demand and somewhat in the Arthur Greenslade mould. A great arranger and 'idea man,' he contributed so much to her success with his interpretation of such songs as 'Girl Don't Come,' 'Long Live Love' and 'Message Understood' — as did Chris Andrews, who wrote many of her hits. A little zany, with her bare feet and emotional entanglements, Sandie was good to work with and approached her singing in a very professional manner.

I have especially happy memories of '(There's) Always Something There to Remind Me', where my fuzz tone guitar is very prominent. I also liked working on 'Girl Don't Come.' and have a funny recollection of the song from the set of *Ready Steady Go* in 1964. Sandie was the last artist on the show, and there was 'the Queen of the Mods' Kathy McGowan on camera, squeaking 'Please welcome Sandie Shaw with her hit single "Girl Don't Come"...'

Sandie didn't.

Completely misjudging the time, she hadn't even got her dress on when she was announced. I was told this later, I hasten to add. The orchestra, conducted by Les Reed, went round and round the intro until the show ground to a halt and cut to the advertisements. I saw her at a recent Showbiz lunch and she looked quite a lady, full of inner confidence. Somebody told me she was a qualified therapy counsellor and had adopted the Buddhist faith. She was certainly a long way from the emotionally out-of-tune and complex young woman I remember. It seems like a dream, now, but I have an abiding memory of her running down a street crying and with no clothes on, in some upset over a man. There were slightly less dramatic tears in the studio when Millie 'My Boy Lollipop' Small turned up at the studio one day, distraught over some guy. Usually, as her records suggest, she was a bouncy and bubbly little character.

From an earlier generation, Lita Rosa was a real toughie, with a mouth like a sewer. Mind you, as a dance band singer for years, many of them in the busy and hectic world of Ted Heath's line-up, I suppose she'd had to be. In fact she'd once been married to one of Heath's trumpeters, Ronnie Hughes, and he always gave the impression that it had been a life experience he would happily have avoided. I did a bit of work with her and still smart from a bruising encounter at Brighton Ice Rink.

Backstage, we were talking about how many thousands of records she was selling a month, and I had the temerity to say in all innocence: 'Well, you're not selling all that many at the moment, are you?' This was not only undiplomatic and ungallant, but altogether a bad move.

'How dare you fucking talk to me like that, you ———!' she screamed, each word separated by a choice epithet for good measure.

I changed it to a feeble: 'Well, I like your records?' but it was all too late. The stream of profanity continued.

You live and learn.

Musicians

Jimmy Page

'As of 1998, he ranks number 15 in the world's 100 richest rock stars with an estimated worth of £55m. Starting out as a studio session hack, his early guitar licks have featured on the recordings of artists such as Donavan, Tom Jones, P.J. Proby, Joe Cocker, Herman's Hermits, The Rolling Stones, etc. As he was then unable to read music, he was given advice by fellow session guitarist Vic Flick.'
http://www.imdb.com/name/nm0656211/bio

When I first met Jimmy he was young, impressionable and wonderfully enthusiastic about the whole music business. He'd been a founder member of Neil Christian and the Raiders and moved into sessions about 1963. Jimmy had little concept of money and what could happen to it. At that time, the contractors always paid the musicians with cash placed in little brown envelopes. Sometimes I would get cramp in my left leg and discover it was this wad of little brown envelopes in my back pocket stopping the circulation. Having a family to keep, that didn't happen too often. Jimmy on the other hand, would take the packets home to his parents' house and hide them under his mattress. Living with his parents and having very few expenses, he asked me on one occasion what he should do with all the money he had stashed away.

'You have to put it in the bank or someone's going to lift it,' I advised him.

'If I do that they'll know how much I've got and I'll have to pay tax and stuff like that,' he replied with a worried frown.

I think that was the only worry Jimmy had at that stage in his life: what to do with his money. Now he probably has the same worry but on a different scale.

Jimmy's black Les Paul got a terrible pounding as I think it was the only guitar he had for a long time. He coaxed some great sounds out of it, sounds that escaped me when I had my couple of Les Paul's. The musical director, Charles Blackwell, used Jimmy a lot on his recordings, as he did Big Jim Sullivan and me. I have read that Jimmy is down as playing on Dave Berry's 'Crying Game' hit single. Not true. Big Jim and I worked on that recording and even with that there is a controversy. For years Big Jim has maintained that he used a 'wah-wah' pedal for the solo licks but I know he borrowed my DeArmond tone and volume control to get that distinctive effect. This was a pedal with a short commercial life that a player could move up and down for volume and side to side for tone. Changing tone could lead to some amusing gyrations which probably had long term effects on my right ankle, knee, hip and lower back. When I was on tour with the John Barry Seven in the late '50s and early '60s, I used a DeArmond volume control with my right foot that meant I had to stand with all my weight on my left leg. This definitely led to complications in later life.

But back to the 'Crying Game': I can remember as plain as if it were today, getting that pedal out of my bag and giving it to Jim to plug up.

Hank Marvin

> 'Hank himself must have looked back on 1977 with particular satisfaction. In August he was presented with a CBS Arbiter Award for services to the music industry, while in November he issued the album "The Hank Marvin Guitar Syndicate," in which he fronted a formidable array of session guitarists, among them Kevin Peek, Vic Flick and Alan Parker: here was a new and exciting "guitar orchestra" for the '70s. "I was very pleased with that album," Hank reflected. "It was aimed really at guitar players or people who are interested in guitar music."
> **MALCOLM CAMPBELL** *(http://malcolmcampbell.me.uk)*
> **NOVEMBER 2003**

Hank and I worked together a few times, in the EMI recording studios and when we were on the same bill at a concert or television show. I had always been interested in Hank's work as he was mainly connected with Cliff Richard, whose own career I had been involved with from our first meeting in Butlins, Clacton, in 1958.

Hank has had many hit records and albums and a number of illustrious accolades awarded him. Working with him on 'The Hank Marvin Guitar Syndicate,' I realized what a perfectionist he is with his sounds, production and equipment. I wish my guitar chords had always been as clean as his! Hank set out from the North of England with his friend Bruce Welch to conquer the London music scene – and conquer it they did. They met Cliff's manager in the 2Is Coffee Bar and the rest is history.

Hank put his name on a few guitars, and one of the few Vox Electric 12 Strings with 'Hank Marvin' emblazoned on the bridge is in my small guitar collection. Jennings Music, who distributed Vox guitars, was the main importers of Fender Guitars from the USA. I was given a Fender Stratocaster for use with the John Barry Seven and Hank and I were amongst the first users of that wonderful guitar. My first Strat was stolen — or, more accurately, left at the side of the road when I was threatened by some thugs after a gig in London. I dove into my car and roared off only to discover the next morning that, to my horror, there was no guitar, foot pedal or JB7 music. That was one bad experience. However, I bought another guitar from Jennings and recouped the cost of 178 pounds sterling from the insurance. Amazing how much one can remember when faced with the loss of the entire JB7 guitar pad. Ray Russell, who followed me into the Seven, had to memorize the guitar music from recordings — and he did a fine job.

Big Jim Sullivan

'Vic Flick was a close companion on many sessions in the 60's. We used to play chess in the moments we had in between takes. I owe quite a lot to Vic, he would help me when the reading was a bit more than I could handle. He showed me how to read phrasing and more important how to read music rests. He would say it's easy to read the notes but to read the rests is more important. Flick was among the handful of top session guitarists in England during the early 1960s when the whole concept of electric guitar as a lead instrument caught fire. Generally, the only available guitarists who could read were trained in classical or jazz and they weren't interested in playing sessions with a 'rocking' feel. This gave rise to a whole generation of players, especially in Britain, who contributed guitar parts to recordings ranging from The Kinks to Engelbert Humperdinck. In addition to Vic Flick, these session men included the likes of Jimmy Page and Big Jim Sullivan.'
http://bigjimsullivan.com/vicflick.html

Big Jim Sullivan was a natural and his ever-inquisitive mind led him to explore the possibilities of the guitar as, at least to my knowledge, no one else has. Judy and I spent one memorable evening in Jim's house where Jim played sitar and swapped licks with Hank Marvin, who was also experimenting with the instrument. I was on tambour, a sort of Indian droning bass. Stamina was the keyword for playing that instrument as it was backdrop for all the whizzing about the two front line players did. Brian Bennett was on tablas and, as is the custom with this type of music, the whole thing went on for about three quarters of an

Big Jim Sullivan

hour. Not being too enthused with this abundance of ethnic outpouring, Judy and I exchanged glances when Jim said, 'Let's play that back!'

As Jim lived at that time in North London, and we lived very much in South of London, we used that as an excuse to beat a hasty retreat before another 'recording' took place. The whole Indian thing took the business over for a few months with sitars of every kind appearing in recording studios. Being large and awkwardly shaped, no cases were available for the authentic version of the sitar. Jim and other exponents would turn up with what resembled a homeless person draped in a blanket stuck under their arm.

Clive Hicks was in great demand with his electric sitar. It was a strange, guitar-shaped instrument with a rack of open strings on the body which resonated with any notes that were played. After being featured on a flurry of hit records, it eventually disappeared along with the acoustic version.

Chris Spedding (of 'Motorbikin' hit-record fame) is a very quiet, introverted kind of guy. He is also a talented guitarist who could fit in with nearly all types of recording. I say nearly, because orchestral guitar wasn't Chris' forte. Any type of small group — Pop, Rhythm and Blues, Country, Rock and Roll, even Heavy Metal — was where Chris shone. Chris had the 'long hair and studded leather jacket' kind of hippie image that went with his guitar style around the period of his hit record, 'Motorbikin.' Years later I arranged to meet Chris in The Kings Head pub in Santa Monica, California. Standing at the bar looking about for Chris, I was surprised when this trim, well-dressed gentleman approached me.

'Ullo, Vic,' the trim, well-dressed gentleman said.

It was the new Chris; I hadn't recognized him at all. Later, of course, after the initial shock had worn off, it was the Chris I had known those years ago and we had a very pleasant evening reminiscing over a few pints.

By complete contrast, bassist Alan Weighell who worked on hundreds of recordings, started to lose his hair at an early age and could best be described as balding. Alan and I were in the rhythm section recording the backing tracks for a French artist. The producer couldn't make the first days recording and arrived early the second day to listen to the previous day's work. The engineer at PYE Studios close to Marble Arch was Ray Prickett who relates the following:

The French producer was listening to the tracks as the musicians started to arrive for the day's work. He was very pleased with the playing and the sounds — especially complementing the bass. Looking through the control room window in Studio 2, the producer suddenly asked, 'Who is that bald man?'

'That's Alan, the bass player,' Ray replied.

'The bass player?' the Frenchman shouted. 'I cannot work with bald bass players. Where is the man from yesterday?'

To the Frenchman's embarrassment Ray said, 'He *was* the bass player from yesterday.'

Guitarist George Kish suffered the same fate at the discriminatory hands of Dusty Springfield. Her cry of, 'I cannot work with bald musicians,' sent George packing and a hastily called hairy replacement scurrying into the studio.

How times have changed!

Through the Adam Faith sessions and John Barry, I was introduced to some great guitar players. On 'Made you,' which we recorded in May of 1960, Adam wanted Joe Brown to play some of his distinctive guitar licks. Into EMI 2 came this young man with tousled blonde hair and an ever present smile. To counter the fact that Joe couldn't read music, something that didn't stop him playing some wonderful guitar, the sound engineer put his amplifier in an isolation booth. Separated from the rest of the band, if Joe came in at the wrong time or played for too long his sound could be adjusted in the control room. As far as I was aware, this precaution wasn't needed and the recording was completed.

'Made You' was used in the film *Beat Girl* and, along with 'When Johnny Comes Marching Home,' went on to become a double A side hit for Adam in June of 1960. I had the pleasure of working with Joe on a few sessions and on many television shows when he appeared as a solo artist and with 'The Bruvvers.'

The sound peculiar to Adam Faith's early records was produced by four violin players plucking their strings in unison. All four were grouped around one microphone. These players, and any others, were assembled by a gentleman named Syd Margo. I don't use the term 'gentleman' lightly because that is exactly what he was. Syd was always immaculately dressed, very courteous with his dealings with musicians and meticulous in his business affairs. Syd's appearance on the John Barry scene happened like so many others in the business — purely by chance. John Barry said to me and Les Reed, who was now in the band, 'How do I get hold of some violin players for this record?'

I didn't know any, except the guy up the street who didn't sound too good, but Les remembered that his uncle had spoken of a friend of his who played violin somewhere in London. Syd's 'phone number was passed to John Barry and contact was made. Shortly afterwards John's fame as an arranger and composer grew, the orchestras grew as the films and record dates rolled in and, one must presume, Syd's bank balance and prestige within the business grew in like manner. His suits certainly got more expensive looking. The saying 'Life is just a 'phone call away' is certainly true.

On the JB7 Plus-Four records and the Adam Faith records, the four violinists were Syd Margo, Bernard Monshin, Alec Firman and Charlie Katz. There must be quite a few musicians who are smiling after reading the names of that quartet. It's interesting to note that as the music business in general exploded so did the working partnership of our very own 'Fab Four.' As JB moved on from the plucking violins, so did the plucking violins move away from each other. Becoming influential contractors in their own right, those four musicians were rarely, if ever, seen in one another's company. Because of the demand for guitar players, I was fortunate enough to work a great deal for Bernard, Syd and Charlie. I worked for Alec to a much lesser extent. Alec had his own thing going with the BBC and was very good at looking after musicians' residual payments for distribution at a later date — a very much later date! In fact the Musicians' Union, following an inquiry, had to pick the date for him! One day I received a cheque for several hundred pounds from the Firman organization with a note attached: 'Please check the enclosed amount against your records and notify this office of any discrepancies.' As none of the musicians were in a position to have access to any information from which to make our records, I settled for the amount offered — as I believe all the other musicians did. At that time, and for many years after, my colleagues and I were completely unaware of how much we were being ripped off by the powers that be.

An orchestra fixed by Alec had gathered in the BBC Shepherds Bush Theatre for a date when one of the Production Assistants came into the orchestra room and announced that Alec Firman had been taken into hospital. A voice from the back of the orchestra asked, "Nothing trivial, I hope?'

The JB7 musicians went to a film studio in Beaconsfield to record the music track for *Beat Girl*, one of John Barry's first film scores in 1960 and a film that featured the up-and-coming star, Adam Faith. Once the sessions got under way the difference in recording techniques became painfully and aurally obvious. Here we all were set up on several large throw rugs or carpets in an enormous sound stage. The stage was so large that John Cameron could have shot the whole of *Titanic* without going outside. The recording engineer moved amongst us setting up microphones, connecting cables to wall outlets and other technical maneuvers. The microphone that was dangling in front of my amplifier was at least six feet away and looked like one of those bombs with a long curly sputtering fuse that spies use in cartoons. We commented on the microphone placement in general and were told in a nice but firm manner to mind our own business.

Comes the playback and all was revealed. The drums sounded like they were in the next county. My guitar sound had lost all its energy and depth. The overall sound was disastrous. After we had gathered in the control room and listened to the playback, the recording engineer settled back in his worn chair, surveyed his knobs, and said, 'How about that, then?' Silence reigned for a few long moments. John Barry, not one to mince his words said, 'We'll have to make some changes here.' And changes were made. Microphone positions moved, perspectives altered, until a sound with some dynamic punch was obtained. Of course, after the adjustments, any semblance of an amicable relationship between 'them' and 'us' ceased to exist. However, the job got done and JB was on his way to film-composing stardom. We all reassembled in EMI Studio Two some days later to record the same music for the album. The influence of the Pop world and brilliant and innovative recording engineers like Malcolm Addey, John Richards and Joe Meek, appeared to be passing by the techniques of the big film studio sound stages. When those sound stages found their work started going to independent recording studios with 'telecine,' or film video playback capabilities, they soon brought themselves, their equipment and techniques up to date.

There are many anecdotes about the 'big' fixers, or contractors of that era. Charlie Katz, Sid Sax, Harry Benson, Sid Margo and Alec Firman had a grip on the greater majority of the recording, television and radio work that was going on in London, and to a lesser extent, in the provinces. Very often I would arrive home after several days of continuous session work and tell Judy to put a line in the diary through the next weekend. I just had to have the time off. Usually, within a few hours, Charlie would call and book in 10 a.m. to 10 p.m. on both days. If you started turning down work for people like Charlie they would assume you didn't want it and would stop calling. It was a kind of 'arm up the back' situation, but you learned to live with it. In one instance a cello player had told Charlie that he was going to be on holiday for two weeks some time in the future. By chance, Charlie dialed his number while he was supposed to be away and the luckless musician answered the phone.

'Oh, I've just remembered,' Charlie said. 'Aren't you supposed to be away?'

'I am just having two weeks at home,' the cellist replied.

'Well, if you want time at home, you can have it,' Charlie responded — and didn't call him again for a whole year.

To emphasize the hardness that could creep into the business, let me tell you a story about a truly fine bass player by the name of Frank Clarke. Frank was taken suddenly ill with a very serious renal disorder and had to be rushed to hospital. The doctors later told his wife, Peggy, that Frank's life was on the line. Peggy called Sid Sax and explained the situation and, because of the near terminal nature of his illness, Frank wouldn't be able to make that afternoon's session.

'Very short notice, isn't it?' Sid said, before putting the 'phone down.

Jim Sullivan and I were in the gents' rest room at Audio International, Rye Muse, Baker Street, when Harry Benson came in. Harry hadn't been booking Jim and me recently so we asked what the matter was. In his inimitable upfront fashion, Harry replied, 'You two are too busy to do my work. It's not worth me calling you.'

'You could at least try, Harry,' Jim said.

'Trying costs me money and you're making too much already,' Harry retorted as he walked out.

Many years later Harry moved down to the South Coast in an effort to retire but he was still asked to fix the odd few sessions. He would call from Brighton and say, 'Vic, I've got some work for you. Call me back.' I suppose Harry figured if you wanted the work you should pay for the call. After all, it was long distance from Brighton to London and money was money!

Actually, Harry was a wonderful character who would take as much verbal as he gave. I'm sure he looked upon musicians as a commodity, like a sack of potatoes, who could either do the work or who couldn't do the work. Everything else, including the verbals, was incidental. Frank Clarke had a dispute with Harry over a payment due on a session. It was just a couple of pounds, but enough for Harry to fight for. If Frank answered the 'phone when Harry called, Harry would ask to speak to Frank's wife, saying he couldn't do business with Frank. This 'war' went on for months. Frank never got his money, but he kept working for Harry.

Eric Ford tells the story of when Harry called him back in the 1960s and asked, 'I can't get anybody for this session. This Vic Slick, is he any good?'

As Eric said to me, 'What was I supposed to say? I corrected your name and said you played OK.'

Never the epitome of tact, Harry once said to me, as I'm sure he has said to others, 'Thank God you can do this date; I've tried everybody else!'

Musicians of the caliber to work in the major recording studios have to have a very professional and responsible attitude to their work. Having earned the confidence of many of the top musicians in the London scene, I often heard them talk of their disappointment at having a cracked trumpet note or a squeak from a saxophone reed accepted on the final take. Although the mistake probably went unnoticed at the time, a musician's performance is nevertheless a very personal thing, and nothing less than perfection is acceptable. I have anguished over mistakes or buzzing strings that seemed to me to stand out like a clap of thunder in the final mix. When I got up enough courage to mention it, no one had noticed a thing.

One morning at CTS in Wembley, I was recording the music for a documentary film for the Jersey Tourist Board. Exploiting the delights of Guernsey with its beaches and other attractions, there was a scene where the camera explored a resident's garden full of exotic plants and bird life. I had written some gentle music that fitted the delicate beauty of the flowers and the birds. The music cue was uncomplicated and was scheduled for very near the end of the session. With another couple of cues to record, I didn't want to spend too much time on it. Over a soft backing of strings, the acoustic guitar played a single note line throughout the cue. It fitted very well. John Richards, the sound engineer, called down to say the recording was good and to move on to the next cue. Walking toward me across the studio floor, clutching his acoustic guitar was Les Thatcher, a fine and respected guitarist. He had a worried expression on his face. 'I buzzed on a note very badly. Could we do it again?

I checked my watch and said we might have time to record the piece again at the end of the session. Of course we didn't, and the extraneous noise stayed in. Every time I saw Les, he would question me about the note.

'Was it very noticeable?'

'Could they edit it out?'

'Did the director say anything about that buzz I made?'

Poor Les was becoming paranoid about this event. It seemed to be starting to take his life over. Some weeks later I saw the editor after the final dub and asked him if he had noticed this buzz on the guitar and explained how serious the incident had become to Les. The editor searched his memory and said, 'Oh, that. Yes, I remember now. I did notice something on the music track so I put a parrot squawk over it. You can't hear a thing now!'

Relating this comment to Les finally broke the spell, and from that day on Les and I had this private joke that if either one of us made a mistake when working together we would say, sometimes in unison: 'Be OK with the parrot on it!'

Mike Leander was an arranger who had several big hits to his name in the mid-to-late 'sixties. He was one of the lucky numbers of whiz kids who were given the run of the studios and, it would seem, unlimited use of musicians. His ideas, enthusiasm and inspiration far outweighed his technical prowess — ideas and inspiration being the currency of the moment. On one date with Mike in Decca 2, there was a wonderful example of both his talents. Walking into the studio with a pile of music parts, fresh from the copyist, Mike proceeded to distribute the parts to the assembled musicians. Approaching Don Honeywell, one of the world's best baritone sax players, as he was in the process of warming up, Mike said the immortal words: 'What instrument do you play?'

Don replied, 'Saxophone!'

'Oh!' said Mike, looking at the pile of parts; 'Which one?'

I can't remember which artist or song it was, but with Mike's magic touch it undoubtedly became a hit.

Another Mike Leander story concerned every guitar player in London Town — except me! (This must have happened during my very busy period.) Day after day, guitarists I found myself working with would ask me if I was booked at Decca 3 on such and such a date. I would say that I was working for the BBC at their Maida Vale, Delaware Road Studios. Time and again, I was asked this same question until I thought it was some kind of set up. The date in question came and went and it transpired that Mike Leander had transcribed one of the Brandenburg Concertos for about thirty guitars and was trying to make a Pop record out of it. Originally described by Bach as '*Six Concerts Avec plusieurs Instruments,*' it was now '*Avec plusier guitars.*' Some of the parts are difficult enough on the instruments they were written for, so when written for the guitar and played by guitarist — some of whose reading ability was suspect under the best conditions — the project was on a course for disaster. Mike had mistakenly assumed that all guitar players who worked in studios could read music. Not so. Very few guitarists could read well enough to even attempt the parts that Mike put in front of them. Mike had put 'Studio Flavors of The Month' on the various lead desks — like Jimmy Page and Mike Eagan, good players but not strong readers. Consequently, as the story goes, there was much shuffling of desks amongst the many guitarists. Confusion reigned for many minutes as guys clamored for the back desks where, with volumes low and heads down, they could gracefully and audibly retire from the proceedings. No one wanted the high profile front desks. Reports that filtered back to me indicated that the session sounded like a mass individual practice session, with not one usable take being made. Was I happy I escaped that session!

However, I didn't escape the Longine Watch sessions. The Longine Company sponsored the recording of albums for inclusion in their catalogues. Of various styles, the albums were always of the highest quality. The producer decided he wanted an album featuring guitars playing in sections, a kind of Les Paul in stereo, with one section answering the other. Not being totally aware of what was involved with the nearly two weeks of work, I was pleased to see many of my fellow guitarists gathered that first morning at Audio International Studios. Judd Proctor, Bryan Daly, Ernie Shear, Colin Green, Terry Walsh, Jim Sullivan, Les Thatcher and I were some of the guitarists who made up the two sections that would be heavily featured throughout the sessions. With bass, drums, keyboard, percussion and other various front line instruments, the studio was quite full.

Unlike the other multi-guitar session referred to earlier, these Longine sessions were being efficiently organized by Ronnie Hazlehurst. Ronnie was the Musical Director of many BBC television shows and his experience was invaluable in smoothing out what could have been a chaotic few days. No scrabbling for the best desks or scuffling off to the back on these sessions. All the parts had each guitarist's first name and each player was assigned a desk — and that's where you stayed. We set up, took our seats and opened the pads of music. Silence fell upon the luckless participants as we surveyed the mass of music we were destined to plough through. After an exchange of horror-filled glances and one or two softly expressed expletives, it was volumes to zero and get stuck in.

Some of the parts were difficult. It was an ambitious project as guitarists very rarely get to play as a section and certainly never eight players at the same time. Realizing that new territory was being charted, Ronnie tactfully concentrated on other studio concerns. How was the percussion set up? Where would the woodwind sit? Were the screens in the right place? Diplomatically, Ronnie gave us time to gather our musical wits and to look over many of the tricky phrases that we were to encounter. A whole galaxy of Britain's top arrangers had been commissioned to write for this combination: Max Harris, Ken Thorne, Roland Shaw and Angela Morley, to name just a few.

As I can remember it, the first day's arrangements had been done by Ronnie himself. He had a good working knowledge of writing for the guitar so, although difficult, the notes made sense. In Henry Mancini's classic book on arranging, Henry advises that the guitar is a 'no man's land' for someone who doesn't play, so write what you hope for and leave it to the player. The first few run-throughs were a bit shaky, but as our brains and fingers got into gear the sessions progressed smoothly.

Of course, not all arrangers were good guitar writers and there was a bit of 'I'll show 'em' going on. Some of the parts we were presented with were horrendous. Phrases that play easy on a flute or a violin can present quite a challenge on the guitar, especially when you are virtually sight reading everything. One morning, having played one piece several times, I realized that the fret board below the 10th fret was cold — all the frets above it were warm from permanently playing around the 11th to 17th fret. There was none of that cozy 'open "E" and "A" strumming' on these sessions. At the end of the project we all came away as consummate sight readers. As one player observed, 'I could read fly shit on a postage stamp at a hundred yards and get it right first time.'

I tried to get copies of the recordings from Ronnie but he had been told that following those sessions, Longine had changed their policy and stopped the music-recording side of their activities. All those tapes are lying in a vault somewhere and as of this writing have probably never been listened to.

A similar occurrence for Readers Digest involved me as musical director. I had just produced a session at Lansdowne of my own material and was hoping to sell it to various library music companies.

At the same time I was doing a lot of recording for Readers Digest on guitar with sessions produced by Chuck Gerhardt. I spoke to Chuck one day and asked him if he would be interested in recording any of my titles for RD. Chuck wanted to hear them and, to my amazed pleasure, called to say he wanted to record all eight titles. They were just perfect for fillers in his up-and-coming project. I put the 'phone down and stared at it for a good few minutes. To arrange and record your own title for Readers Digest was a good thing. To arrange and record eight of your original titles was unheard of. On top of that, orchestrations for a sixty-piece orchestra were not usually given to Pop guitarists. Each arrangement took me a long time. I wanted no mistakes and I want each one to be interesting, commercial and musical.

The sessions went well. With Chuck producing and musicians in the orchestra such as Don Lusher, Derek Watkins, Greg Bowen, Roy Willox, Dave Richmond — and a string section led by Syd Sax — everything was in my favour. After the recordings were completed, there followed all the usual contract signing. Readers Digest insisted on the 'penny rate' for mechanical sales. I was happy to sign as the sale of all Readers Digest albums were in the millions.

Again, I thought, 'This is it. I've cracked it. Big time, here I come. Order the Yacht!'

I checked with Chuck a few weeks later to find out how the albums were coming together and when they would be issued. Chuck then told me that Readers Digest production had been taken over by an equally professional producer, Joe Habig. All Chuck's recent productions were being archived.

I don't know how many professional highs and lows a person is expected to experience in his life time but I think I've had my quota. Still, I gave everything my best shot and that's all you can do. I've been lucky with too many things to be affected long term by bad news. To compensate in some measure for the disappointment, I did get to record with Harry James for Readers Digest. He was someone I had admired all my life. What a professional person he turned out to be!

When an arranger gets to be as busy and as good as Nelson Riddle, he has to take some short cuts. Joe Habig, having taken over from Chuck, came over to the rhythm section with a score by Nelson Riddle.

'Have a look at this,' Joe said.

Written on the score, just above the saxophone line were the words: 'Proper five-part harmony this time. Not the shit you threw at me last time.'

Being Nelson Riddle, you have to excuse him anything.

A good example of how 'dog eat dog' the music business can be is my opportunity to write the music for the exclusive documentary of the 1966 World Cup Football held in England. I had written quite a few music scores for the company and the editor that was involved with the film so I was pleased to be told that I was up to do the music. Would I prepare a costing and be ready to view the rough cut?

I did and I was!

Many days went by and I called the editor to check out what was happening.

'Oh,' he said. Johnny Hawksworth's doing it.'

'*What*!' I moaned. 'How much for? Did I over quote?'

'He's doing it for nothing,' came the reply. 'He's doing it just for the royalties.'

As the obvious and ridiculous next step was to pay to write the music, I decided to put that one down to experience.

Johnny was the bass player for the celebrated Ted Heath Orchestra and there were many stories concerning his quirks. Allow me to relate a couple.

Whenever the band hit a new airport, there would always be several announcements such as: 'Would Mr. Johnny Hawksworth please pick up the nearest white telephone for an important message?' or, 'Mr. Hawksworth, please call your office as soon as possible.' Intrigued by these messages, some of the musicians followed Johnny and found he would skulk off as soon as he arrived at an airport and head for the nearest pay phone and page himself. I suppose he got some mysterious pleasure from doing that.

One of the show numbers that involved Johnny with the Ted Heath band was 'Big Noise from Winnetka.' The production involved Johnny and his bass moving to front of stage and drummer Ronnie Verral following him and playing rhythms on the strings of the bass. Before I relate the rest of this story, I have to say that the band had been on tour for several weeks and in those days of yore — the 1950s — places to attend to personal hygiene and laundry were few and far between. So, picture the scene, the band in the background, Johnny and Ronnie up front with the microphone and Ted Heath getting ready to count the number in. Mr. Heath then asked the question he wished he hadn't asked, 'Johnny, why don't you play the bass with your toes?'

Leaping to any showbiz type challenge, Johnny tore off his shoes and peeled off his socks (peeling being the operative word). Holding the socks up like the Olympic Torch, they were handed from bass player to band leader with a flourish. Ronnie Verral swears, that apart from the smell being horrific, the socks were actually alive! The shocked and repulsed look on Ted Heath's face was one of the better parts of the production. Counting the band in and dropping the socks almost immediately, Ted Heath retreated to back of the stage, leaving poor Ronnie to play his rhythms and avert his nose as far as possible from the rotting socks.

Ah, the romance of touring!

Fashions come and go in everything, from cars, to clothes, to food. The same thing happens with musical instruments. In the mid-'sixties, hit records coming from the USA were featuring the marvelous organ sound of the Hammond B3. The organ filled out and gave a depth to Pop records that was as effective as, and much cheaper than, a string section. My good friend Kenny Salmon decided to buy a Hammond B3 and try to get all the work on that instrument sown up. As it happened, he did very well with work on the Hammond which, in a way, was a shame because the world was denied his excellent piano playing.

As large and big as the sound of the instrument was, it was equally large and big to move about. Not only was it heavy, it was extremely awkward in shape and size. Harold Smart, a renowned exponent of the organ, would hire street workers or construction workers to move his instrument in and out of studios. When we recorded 'World without Love" with Peter and Gordon in EMI 2, Abbey Road, Harold had hired four city road workers to lift the organ into the studio. Like the bearers of some Egyptian Pharaoh, each man had hold of one end of two poles that supported the organ. Looking about them in awe as they slowly entered the studio, they were in great danger of tripping over the many cables and microphone stands. Their dusty figures and muddy boots were in stark

1962 Vox Electric 12 String. Not the easiest instrument to work with, but heard prominently on Peter and Gordon's "World Without Love."

contrast to the studio interior. I suppose if you've spent the major part of your life operating a pneumatic drill in the open air one would be very aware of the intricacies and technicalities of a recording studio. However, the road workers were so fascinated by the inside of EMI 2 and all its paraphernalia that we had a hard time getting them to leave. Those men hung around the studio for three hours waiting to take out Harold's Hammond. No holes got dug in St Johns Wood roads that afternoon.

Back to Kenny Salmon's B3: Of the sessions that Kenny and I worked on, many were at Lansdowne Studios — the 'Achilles' Heel' of all musicians with heavy and awkward shaped instruments. The studio was situated in the double basement of an old house on Lansdowne Road, Bayswater. There was a small elevator that, try as we might, we could not get the Hammond B3 in. The only alternative was to carry it down one flight of fire escape stairs to the control room level then down another flight of stairs to the studio level.

Thinking back on it, I suppose we could have left Kenny on the first level and kept in contact with a head set. I don't know exactly why, but I used to get lumbered with helping Kenny down all these flights of stairs with this damn organ. Heaving and struggling with this monster left Kenny and me breathless and exhausted even before the session had begun. The metal handles that had been bolted to the ends of the B3 to ease its handling — so the brochure read — cut deep grooves into our fingers. My fingers took a good few minutes to return to any semblance of playing condition. Many years later I came to understand the foolishness of what I was doing to my hands. Sensing the future held little comfort if he was to carry on as he was, Kenny had the bloody thing cut in half. This lightened the load somewhat but didn't increase my enthusiasm for helping him. Even cut in half, we still couldn't get the thing into the elevator.

How we used to envy pianists like Ronnie Price! He would walk in at the last minute and the most physical effort they did was to open the piano lid. Later, of course, as fashion once again dictated, Ronnie would come to work with the necessary Prophet Synthesizer and attendant pedals and cables.

Trying to keep up with the sounds of tomorrow, pianists were trying everything, from the Clavioline to the Farfisa Organ and the Vox Organ — famous for its sound on Procul Harum's 'Whiter Shade of Pale.' Another 'innovative' keyboard was the Clavioline. This appendage to the keyboard of a piano gave off a strangulated buzzing noise that was, for instance, heavily featured on 'Telstar' by the Tornados. Only a genius such as Joe Meek could have turned such an aberration into a hit sound. Anyway, a funny story about a Clavioline and pianist, musical director

Ted Taylor took place at EMI's studio during a John Barry instrumental session. John had this idea of duplicating the high string line with a similar sound on the Clavioline. This gave the recording something that nobody else had — or maybe even wanted! Imagine Studio 2 full of string players, the rhythm section at the back against the wall and Ted Taylor in the dreaded soloist position (the very position I had occupied

Pianist Ronnie Price and Vic working on something!

during the recording of the album *Stringbeat*). One of the characteristics of the Clavioline was the extremely light touch that was needed to work the keys.

To demonstrate this, Ted would blow on the keys with his mouth and try to play a tune. We would make out that this couldn't be so and chide him into giving prolonged demonstrations of his newfound technique. On this particular occasion, someone had bet him that he couldn't play this awful instrument by blowing on the keys through his nose. Ever one to take on a bet, Ted bowed over his chosen instrument and tried to play what sounded like one part of 'Chopsticks' with his left nostril. Halfway though this Command Performance, John Barry called the orchestra to readiness. The Red Light was illuminated. So here we were: A full orchestra of the finest musicians in town, instruments at the ready and all staring at Ted Taylor blowing down his nose and trying to play 'Chopsticks' on this buzzing machine — completely oblivious to his surroundings. Only when Ted started to run out of oxygen and surface to the pregnant silence of the studio that he realised what a foolish sight he must have been. Ever red of face and blustery, Ted surpassed himself in his apologies to John Barry and the orchestra in general. He won the bet!

A competitor in the 'new sound' department was the Farfisa Organ. It had eighty-eight notes and was painted green and arrived in the UK around 1965. One great advantage was that it weighed about one quarter of a Hammond B3 but had nowhere near the quality of sound. Arthur Greenslade bought himself one of these Farfisas and, as an arranger, proceeded to write its various sounds into all the arrangements he did, spurred on, no doubt, by the extra money he got for porterage bringing the machine with him.

One fine day at the end of the session and again at Lansdowne, Arthur allowed John, the studio attendant, to carry his Farfisa up the two flights of stairs and leave it on the pavement for Arthur to put in his car. Lansdowne Studios had realized that help was needed to gain access to the studio level. The good thing about John the studio attendant was that he was very willing and friendly and strong. The not-so-good part was that for the majority of the time his thoughts were back in his native Barbados. Struggling up the stairs with the green monster and finally reaching the pavement, John lent this precious instrument against the railings that surrounded the studio fire escape. His mind obviously elsewhere, he took as little attention to the steepness of the angle he had set the organ at as he had the very windy conditions of the day. As Arthur's head came level with the pavement, he witnessed the horrifying spectacle of his beloved money-making machine being blown flat onto the unforgiving flagstones. I was right behind him and did a double cringe as I heard the sickening crash of the organ hitting the stone and Arthur's shriek of dismay. I also witnessed the clattering, crashing and splintering sound as the Farfisa's inner workings slid down to one end of the instrument as Arthur stood it on end. By the time Arthur had finished shouting and gesticulating, John was certainly wishing he was back in Barbados. The Farfisa, now a complete write off, was happily never seen again.

More Television

On one TV show with the orchestra led by the indomitable Alyn Aynsworth, I found myself confronted with 'The Rodrigo Guitar Concerto,' not a piece to be taken lightly at any time. Sight reading Alyn's version with its written spread chords and long, fast runs was not a task to be flippant about and, believe me, I was not at all flippant. As one has to do in these situations, you get your head down, engage automatic pilot and go for it — hoping that the years of playing experience lets you set the right course. After a couple of run-throughs, Len Shorey, a respected BBC sound engineer, suggested a take. With one or two minor glitches and the occasional string buzz, the title was in the can. Very relieved, I sat back and relaxed. I assumed that the title was for a production number, a moody dance sequence, or a montage of camera shots. It turned out that I was the moody montage that the cameras would be focusing on!

We get to the studio the next day and the Floor Manager asked what height stool I wanted to sit on.

'What do you mean? What height stool?' I inquired.

'For your solo with the guitar thing,' he said, a half-smile flitting across his face. It was then that I discovered I was to mime to the recording we had made the previous day. The edge was very quickly taken off the day!

Rehearsals went OK with just a few 'Are you sure you can hear the track, Vic?' Just a subtle way Len had of saying I hadn't quite got my fingers together with the music. (Before you say anything, you try it! Recording the music one day and trying to play it exactly as you had on camera the next — without the music to guide you — is challenging indeed.)

Came the time of the show and the dreaded cry of, 'Vic — on the set, please!' With faltering steps, I made my way to the electric chair — that is, stool. I sat and waited. It must have been only seconds before the music was cued when Ronnie Price, a wonderful pianist, called from the ranks of the orchestra: 'Vic, your belt's not in its loops correctly. Don't let your trousers fall down!' That helped break the tension of the moment and I went on to do a favourable performance.

'What the hell?' Ronnie said afterwards. 'I could see you wanted loosening up.'

He didn't know how close I was to being too loose. There's a saying in the session business, or probably any interactive business: 'You're either bored to death or scared to death.'

How true that is!

A far less delicate incident happened on one of the *Ready Steady Go* TV shows. 'RSG,' as the show was fondly known, was the 1963 Associated Rediffusion TV's answer to other Pop TV shows like *Oh Boy* and *Drumbeat*. Twinkle, who boasted extremely large mammary glands, had a hit song called 'Terry' and was booked to appear. The director had placed Twinkle on a small stage against a white muslin back drop. With the studio darkened and a spot light focused on her, the revealing outline was all-too-clearly silhouetted on the white back drop. Two stagehands were at the back of the small stage presumably holding the muslin taut and very much aware of the silhouette. What the two men weren't aware of was that the boom microphone was on and pointing at Twinkle and, unfortunately, directly at them.

'Christ! Joe. Look at them tits!' reverberated around the studio, as one of the luckless duo admired Twinkle's physical attributes.

The floor manager, in a very professional way, brought order to the studio by shouting at the top of his voice: 'Quiet on the set — and that means you two behind the back drop!'

Twinkle seemed to enjoy her moment of soft porn fame and thrust herself into the song.

Phil Coulter and Bill Martin were a team of very successful song writers who had written a song for Twinkle, the one she was plugging on *Ready Steady Go*. Twinkle's other claim to fame, apart from her mammary glands, is she must be the only singer who is not listed on *Google*.

Michael Parkinson had his own very successful chat show in the 1970s. The band for the first few years was led by keyboard and organist legend, Harry Stoneham. Jim Lawless on percussion, Pete A'Hern on drums, Pete Morgan on bass and me on guitar made up 'The Harry Stoneham Quintet.' Parkinson had some very prestigious guests which made his show a 'must watch' for the British viewing public.

One of those guests was the American movie star, James Stewart. Because he was only available for the morning, the Parkinson Show used the set for another TV show, a set which necessitated the band being set up high on a rostrum. After playing the theme tune for the show, Parkinson introduced his special guest. Being an exclusive interview, there was nothing else to play until the theme at the end of the show. That's a long time stuck up high under the hot lights of the studio with Mr Stewart's sleep-inducing monotone drawling away for the better part of an hour. All this coupled with the director's continual insistence before the show for complete silence made for a dangerous scenario.

It was a scenario to which I readily succumbed. I fell asleep only to

In Phillips Studio with, from left to right, Vic, Bryan Daly, Bill Martin, Phil Coulter and Twinkle.

be startled into wakefulness by a loud and clanging open string guitar chord. My guitar had fallen from my lap onto my foot volume control before hitting the floor. In the silence of the studio the noise was catastrophic. Because the set wasn't our usual one, the sound guys had used the space available to give us more room to sit and play. They had also placed my amplifier away from me, separated by the music stand. Suddenly awake, I dove for the source of the sound, knocking my stand over as I grabbed the amplifier's control knob. This made even more noise. The director was now nearly apoplectic. Parkinson's face was registering shock and horror. The band was in hysterics - and Mr Stewart droned on.

Things weren't quite the same after that!

Parkinson made a TV coup by getting Robert Mitchum to appear for an interview. Word from the Mitchum camp was that no mention was to be made or questions asked about drinking to excess or fisticuffs.

Mitchum walked on to the set to rapturous applause, then took his seat and the interview began. After a few pleasantries Parkinson started to get to the nitty-gritty of Mitchum's career, asking questions about co-stars and directors. And then, the unmentionable: 'Do you find, because of your tough image, people want to get you into arguments, or even fights?'

Silence.

Mitchum slowly raised his eyes to meet Parkinson's and said quietly, but with meaning.

'What sort of a dumb question is that to ask me?'

More silence.

Parkinson gathered himself and started asking questions listed on the clipboard clutched in his hand. All he got as answers were 'yes,' 'no' or 'dunno.' The interview ground to a halt sooner than expected and we played a very long version of the theme tune to fill in the dead air.

Parkinson disappeared from the set and after packing up I decided to take Judy and her friend Moira, who'd been in the audience, to the Green Room in a hope of seeing Robert Mitchum. Even though the room was crowded, it was as if there was only one person in it, and that was Mitchum. He was an amazing presence. No wonder he was the star he was. Moira insisted on getting his autograph so, clutching her little book, she made her way to where Robert Mitchum was standing.

'May I have you're autograph, please, Mr Mitchum?' she asked, and then noticed her book was upside down.

'I'm sorry, Mr Mitchum, it's upside down.'

Taking the book from Moira he looked up and said, in that wonderful voice of his, 'What's wrong with upside down?'

Now, that is a Star!

Bing Crosby made one of his last public appearances on Michael Parkinson's show. He was to be interviewed and sing a parody of 'White Christmas.' Surrounded by the director, floor manager and other BBC staff that wanted 'to be there,' the diminutive singer approached the Harry Stoneham Five.

'Hi guys,' he said. 'I haven't sung this song with these words before, could we run it through?' Of course, we were pleased to play anything for this vocal legend. A short intro, then Bing was singing like a good one, following the words on his cue sheet. We finished and Bing continued to look at the paper, mumbling to himself.

'Sorry, guys. Could we run it through one more time?'

Once again we were pleased to accommodate him.

'Well, that will do it, I hope,' Bing said with a smile. 'Thank you.'

After he had been interviewed, sung his song perfectly and the show had come to a finish, Bing Crosby made a point of walking across the studio floor and thanking us again.

Now, that's another Star!

Simon Dee was the classic example of someone who blew it. I personally liked his style — cynical with a hint of sarcasm — but it did upset a lot of his guests. Starting on radio with the offshore 'pirates,' Simon graduated to 'real' radio and then to his own television series. On one particular show his guest was Howard Keel, a very big film star of *Annie Get Your Gun* fame and someone who, I am sure, prided himself on his vocal talents. After singing his heart out on his big number, Howard Keel returned to the interview area and sat down to enthusiastic applause. Simon paused, waited for silence and staring at Howard said, 'Pretty average, Howard, old chap.'

The rest of the interview was as icy as Simon's broadcasting career was short lived.

Everything that goes up must come down was certainly true in Mr Dee's case. The musical director on *The Simon Dee Show* was Max Harris. Like John Pearson, Max, an excellent pianist and arranger, had a record in the Top Ten with 'Gurney Slade.' Also, like John Pearson, Max never made it into the charts with a follow up.

I received a call from Tony Gilbert for a TV date at the BBC Shepherds Bush Theatre 'Just take your cello acoustic guitar,' was the request. I arrived on time and entered the stage door. There were no musicians and everything was quiet.

Uh-oh, I thought, something's wrong here.

I walked onto the stage area and asked a technician, 'Where's the band?'

'*You're* the band, mate,' replied the technician.

I saw some paperwork about the show and found it was an insert for *The Two Ronnie's*, a very popular television comedy. The Manhattan Transfer were going to record 'Java Jive' with just little old me.

Help!

After a few minutes, I seemed to be surrounded by sound guys, camera men, the floor manager and the director.

'Let's run it through,' the director said.

I was given the guitar part from the big band arrangement and, after setting the tempo, off we went. Following the first run-through, the tall girl asked me to play the lead trumpet part throughout the piece as well as playing rhythm. She got her cues from the trumpets, she said. After explaining all I had was chord symbols and no cues of any kind, she mumbled something and returned to the other three singers.

Following the third run-through, the floor manager told me top report to wardrobe. Wow! What was all this about? The ladies in wardrobe fitted me out with a 'Beau Brummel' jacket, a shirt with frills down the front, tights — and what looked and felt like ballet shoes. Having been rehearsed and fitted out, I was told to report back in four hours for the recording. Don't ask me why — that's how TV works.

I called Judy and said I was coming home and I wanted her in the studio for moral support. Back we went to Shepherds Bush, into the theatre and made ready for the show. Setting up, the stagehand said, 'Anyfink yer want, mate?'

'I'd like a music stand for my music, please.'

After looking at his manifest he said, "Aven't got one ordered, mate, but I'll see wot I can do," and disappeared.

The Beau Brummel jacket might look good but it wasn't designed for playing guitar. The material was like a canvas and very unforgiving. I could only bend my right arm so far, which was not the ideal playing position.

A run-through was ordered and now I had my music stand I was ready for action. One run-through with cameras and sound. Another run-through for cameras. Yet another run-through for the Manhattan Transfer. My right arm was starting to go numb.

'Stand by. Manhattan Transfer, Take one!' shouted the floor manager.

Five minutes later...

'Stand by. Manhattan Transfer, Take two!' shouted the floor manager.

My arm was now numb and the pick was falling from my deadened fingers. 'I'll have to have a moment for the blood to come back to my arm and hand,' I pleaded.

It was as if I had shouted 'Fire!' People started rushing about the stage area like headless chickens. A nurse appeared from nowhere asking where the blood was. The Manhattan Transfer looked as if the world had fallen in on them: A musician had the temerity to complain!

We finally got the number in the can and everybody was happy - and I thankfully got dressed in normal clothes. How did those old romantics in the Eighteenth Century do anything in that get up? With stiff jackets, tights with no zip, plus — and I would hazard a guess — an unhealthy dose of body odor, their luck must have been well out!

I asked Judy what she thought of the show.

'You looked very pretty!' she said.

The Walker Brothers were riding high in the charts with their 1965 hit single 'Make it Easy on Yourself,' which I had the pleasure of working on. Simon Dee had invited the Walker Brothers to sing their song on his TV show. Max Harris was the musical director and the band contained such luminaries as Tubby Hayes, Ronnie Ross and — may I say it? — me. Packing up after the show I had made my getaway by rushing off to get my car. I parked in the wilds of Shepherds Bush and left Judy to watch my instruments. When I returned and was putting my gear in the trunk of my car, a distraught woman came up to me.

'Has Tubby left yet?' she asked. 'I desperately need to see him. Please help me. Please? Please?'

Thinking it would take just a minute to point her in the direction of the studio (and Tubby), I said, 'Follow me!'

In the Lime Grove studios, panic had broken out. There was some sort of alarm and before I knew it, the woman and I were directed this way and that and I was lost within the rabbit warren of corridors.

When I reappeared in the street the panic inside had erupted outside, mainly caused by my parked car, containing a stricken Judy, surrounded by BBC heavies. A carefully orchestrated escape by the Walker Brothers to evade the mass of fans gathered in the street had been foiled by my car.

Having just opened the trunk of my car, I had the keys!

The BBC heavies were trying to push my car out of the way so the small Austin Mini containing the Brothers could roar off as planned. Judy was crying, the heavies were swearing, I was sweating and the fans were starting to tear the Mini to bits. I jumped in, started the car and made a hasty exit, followed by the stricken Mini and the Brothers. Getting to the end of Lime Grove Street, I turned right and the Mini turned left. Side by side at the end of the one-way street, I suffered the full vocabulary of epithets the red-faced Mini driver shouted at me. And so ended an unpleasant evening. There was a slight tension when working with the Walker Brothers after that incident, but we all realized we were victims of circumstance.

Another TV show I worked on many times was *Top of the Pops*. This show ran for years on BBC 1 and gave a terrific boost to the careers of all the acts that appeared. One especially memorable show for me featured The Moody Blues. Not requiring an orchestra, as they had previously recorded their own backing, it was a chance for the musicians to sit back and relax. Waiting while the camera operators got their instructions and other rehearsal type business went on, Justin Hayward left the set and walked toward the orchestra. A nervous Johnny Pearson assumed that Justin wanted to talk to him about some musical question. Instead, Justin walked straight passed him and up to my music stand.

'Vic, I have to thank you,' he said
'Thank me? What for?' I asked him.
'It was your playing on TV and records that inspired me to take up the guitar, join a group, and here I am. Thank you.'
With that, he shook my hand and returned to the set. It was a wonderfully warm, fuzzy moment.

Every now and then, I would get booked on a television production that took place outside of London. Towns like Glasgow, Brighton, Eastbourne, Manchester, and Cardiff are amongst the many that played host to musicians from the 'smoke' — and in general treated us very well. In the early 1970s, work was going very well and the family used to take two months' vacation in Florida or on our boat on the South Coast of England. A series of summertime specials had been booked with two of the shows being scheduled back to back right in the middle of my two months. The pay was good so I decided to fly back from Florida, work the shows and fly back to the Sunshine State to continue the holiday. There was the added incentive of, if I didn't do them all I wouldn't do any. One of the musicians asked me which way I came down from London. I replied, 'I've just come from Florida.'
'Oh,' he said. 'I drove down the Brighton Road. The traffic was quite good.'
Wonderful people, musicians.

In the mid-'seventies contractor David Katz has assembled a very large orchestra on the sound stage at Denham Studios on the outskirts of London. Rumour had it that a couple of big stars were to record music for a television show. As the time to start arrived, a cluster of people poured through the studio entrance surrounding a veiled Liza Minnelli.

They swept up the side of the studio and slowed to a halt outside the control room. A moment later a lone Isaac Stern carrying his trusty violin followed the same route and discussions started.

Music was handed out to the orchestra and the rehearsal commenced. The music was a mixture of Broadway and Classical. I couldn't work out what the theme of the show was. Could it be Isaac playing the violin whilst Liza sang, or Liza dancing whilst Isaac played a jig? Whatever it was, the orchestra committed a mixture of music to tape and dispersed. Apart from the money, I never heard of the recording again. I was part of a few 'mystery' sessions that cost a great deal, big names were involved, and of which no trace remains.

Manchester, renowned for its hospitality, didn't let itself down. *The International Pop Proms* was televised from the Belle Vue complex in Manchester, a venue perhaps more famed for its circuses than its television programs. This became very evident in the summer of 1975 when the odor of elephant dung wafted up from the animal enclosures to the orchestra.

Although there were some sixty musicians led by Les Reed and there were 'stars' in abundance from many countries, the highlight, in retrospect, was the locally brewed Boddingtons beer. Dave Richmond (booked on bass guitar) and I went looking for alternate refreshment to that provided by the in-house canteen. We set off down the adjacent street to look for a pub. Except for the odd building sticking up like a tombstone, the area around Belle Vue was, at that time, mostly flattened, with condemned housing being torn down to make way for new Council houses. Fortunately, those odd buildings left standing turned out to be pubs and the one Dave and I entered served Boddingtons beer. The light, tasty beer with a creamy head had long been the staple drink of Mancunians and was soon to become the staple drink of *The International Pop Proms*.

A few years later, musicians in the BBC television orchestra organised a coach outing to visit the brewery. That outing is a separate story all of its own. The small pub that Dave and I found was run by a very pleasant couple who took the business of serving beer and food very seriously. The summer of 1975 was very hot and it took all of the poor landlord's time to keep the beer at its correct temperature of 52-56 degrees Fahrenheit. Air conditioning had not yet reached the wilds of Belle Vue, so down in the cellar the landlord had the large barrels covered in towels which he religiously kept wet with the contents of buckets of cold water. After our first visit, when we had a pint and a meat pie, we returned and told of our find to the other musicians and technicians. The next day there was about eight of us, then fifteen and toward the middle of the series (which ran for eight weeks) there must have been between twenty and thirty people from the show having lunch there. Such business at lunchtime was a rarity for that area and to show his appreciation, the landlord would often drop a couple of free pints off at our table for Dave and me as a kind of 'thank you' for all the trade he was experiencing.

The shows themselves were set on an expansive and expensive set and looked great on the screen. Directed and produced by Johnny Hamp, *The International Pop Proms* proved very successful. I knew Johnny Hamp from many years previous when he was the road manager for the Paul Anka tour. That was the tour on which I met John Barry. Remembering how my father was concerned about my ability to keep a wife, two children, two cars and a house on five days work, brings a particular moment to mind. In 1978 (the year of my father's death, and two years after my mother's passing), I was in the orchestra of a television show when I glanced up at the TV monitor and happened to see a full close up of my face. This wasn't necessarily a shot that would be included in the show but, nevertheless, there it was. Looking up at the monitor this day and seeing my face in close-up brought home to me, with an incredible impact, that my father was no longer with us. He would no longer be seeing me on the 'tele.' No longer be settling down with his cup of tea, biscuits and a pipe of his favourite tobacco to watch a show with the chance of seeing his son strumming away. They say that grief presents itself in many forms and when you least expect it. At that moment, looking up at the monitor, I was overwhelmed with sadness and a weird, space-like kind of loneliness.

The show had to go on, in fact we were in the middle of a routine, but if I could have left the set and found a lonely place to be, I would have cried my heart out. I think my colleagues were concerned when tears started to roll down my cheeks. In fact, I had to stop playing because I couldn't see the music. Perhaps I should have run off the set and not bottled up my emotions. Maybe the director or producer would have understood - but I didn't leave the set, I stayed. Even with my own family that I was so lucky to have, I felt at that moment I was on my own in the big world, that I had truly left the nest.

I miss my mother and father very much. They were always supportive of me and their unconditional love was always there for me, indeed, as it were for my wife Judy and our children, Jayne and Kevin. As parents in the 1950s, it took a lot of heart searching to stand by and watch, as well as encourage, your son to be a professional musician when all they wanted was for me to be a teacher or a doctor — or just anything 'respectable.'

God bless them.

Musicians' Union

Everything is for a purpose. The experience I gathered on social committees came in useful when I had dealings with and later joined the Musicians' Union's various committees. Here I was involved in decisions that directly affected my work. It came as a shock to find out who were sitting on these Musicians' Union committees. Bless their cotton socks and all that, but some committee members' experience in the music world was definitely restricted to blowing 'The Lady is a Tramp' every other Saturday at the local Masonic Hall — and these people were making decisions that affected the incomes and working standards of some of the finest musicians in the world.

Tristan Fry, Chris Gradwell, and I became frustrated at the Musicians' Union's detached attitude toward the session musician so, to more truly represent musicians' needs and problems, we formed The Guild of Professional Musicians. The Guild proved a popular concept and a growing number of musicians attended the meetings. For one meeting, EMI kindly allowed us the use of Studio 1 — such was the interest and the need for the Guild, the Studio was two thirds full of the top London recording musicians.

This was not the first time musicians had banded together in an effort to change the Union's thinking. John Fiddy, Barry Morgan and Les Hurdle had formed the Association of Recording Musicians (ARM). Perhaps the Guild should have been more aware of the Union's reaction to musicians forming such a group, because the members of the Association of Recording Musicians (ARM) were treated and warned in the same way as I am about to describe, although, perhaps, not so severely.

The union had been content to watch all the activities of the guild from a discreet distance until the tide of discontent started to rise a little too quickly. We were told, unofficially, yet in no uncertain terms by a union official Don Smith (affectionately nicknamed 'Dr. Death'), that if the guild continued to function, its members would not be allowed to work in any studio in Great Britain. Don Smith threatened that all other unions involved with recording, television, broadcasting and concerts would be sympathetic to the Musicians' Union ban. A list of names of all participants of the guild would be circulated to all entertainment-related unions — in other words, 'a Black List.' Relations had definitely turned sour.

Many musicians had made generous donations to the guild, donations reflecting the need for an organization concerned with their needs. A pension fund needed to be set up, separate representation was needed, residuals on recordings, investigation of the Phonographic Performance Fund contributions. All these items needed to be discussed by those who were directly affected. At one meeting that was called between the guild and the Musicians' Union Executive Committee, feelings and emotions ran high. After explaining our case yet again, I was called a 'damned subversive reactionary' by a certain executive committee member from the North of England. Naturally, I wasn't going to stand for such an insult to my colleagues and I started to read this gentleman's fortune for him.

After some degree of order had returned, it was put to the guild that if it had articles, then the Musicians' Union would be prepared to look again at its position. Now, Articles of Incorporation don't come out of thin air — they come out of the money the musicians had donated. This money was to finish up in the pockets of Mr Trevor Lyttleton, who took little persuasion to act on our behalf. Trevor was very good and very sympathetic to our cause but, like all legal personnel, very expensive. Let me underline and make it perfectly clear that we only went to this expense because the Musicians' Union insisted on it. Having authorised such an action and spent a great deal of money on legal fees, the union's officials were shouting from the rooftops and using all the avenues available to them to describe how the guild's founders were irresponsible and squandering musicians' money on unnecessary legal fees — forgetting to mention it was Musicians' Union officials who had pressured us into spending the money.

In answer to what was now obviously an overwhelming need, the union set up a 'session section' under the auspices of Don Smith. Musicians were approached who were, without doubt, established session musicians and a Session Section Committee was formed — with yours truly as a member. In an effort to maintain a degree of exclusivity, musicians' names had to be submitted to this committee and their track record reviewed before they could become a member of the Session Section. At every meeting there was a list of names presented to the committee and, at the beginning, they were all accepted. As time passed and the policies and decisions of the Session Section Committee were taking affect, more and more names were being put forward which nobody had heard of. Those musicians' credentials were questioned but whether they were accepted or not, their names would appear on the roster.

Then, without announcement, the procedure stopped. Questioned about this, Don Smith replied that the process was no longer required as the flow of prospective members had almost stopped. At this time there were in the region of 300 names on the list. Several months after members of the Committee had insisted on knowing the number of members, we were told the list had grown to nearly a thousand.

Imagine: From no more than 300 applicants, to nearly a thousand!

Who had been letting these people in? No substantial answer was forthcoming. A couple of years later there seemed to be more people in the session section than there were members of the Musicians' Union. Perhaps this was a ploy by the union's executive committee at that time to disarm the session section by making it unmanageable and return to the peaceful days of yesteryear. One of the reasons for the setting up of a separate section for the recording musicians was that any benefits which had or might arise from being a recording musician would go to the correct people and not be 'lost' in some numbered account the union had a penchant for setting up. With the membership list now completely out of proportion, the whole point of the exercises had been lost. This was later to be proven when the Government Monopolies and Mergers Commission (MMC) investigated the Phonographic Performance Fund's payments to the Musicians' Union and found a great deal lacking in the arrangement. The astonished recipients of the initial payments by the union, payments made only after being ordered by the MMC (and probably under duress) found they were just a few amongst a total of 8,000 session musicians — a totally improbable number.

There is factual proof of significant payments being made to musicians who had only been in studios one or two times. Once a large payment to a completely unknown musician was inadvertently stapled to another much smaller payment made to a well-known musician. The discrepancy in 'famousness' and amount of time spent recording in studios for major artists was mind boggling. Verification of the numbers and the names and amounts received by the session musicians were deemed secret and not for the eyes of the members. Once again, we have the situation of an organisation formed of, by and for the members suddenly becoming a secret society with information being given out on a strictly 'need to know' basis — and it was obviously thought we didn't need to know!

I remember at one session section meeting the subject of residuals being paid to recording musicians was once again brought up. This whole issue was becoming a *raison d'etre* for me and I asked how was it that the Number 2 Account had thousands in it and had been used over the years for pension plans and new cars for union officials when money, earned by recording musicians, was unable to be distributed to those whose right it was to receive it.

'We don't have the mechanics to distribute the money to musicians and, anyway, the money is for the general betterment of the Music Business in general,' was the response from the General Secretary.

The 'Betterment of the Music Business' manifested itself as donations to such diverse recipients as tambourine bands in Truro, jazz bands in Bridlington, extraordinarily large 'loans' to orchestras that were eventually 'written off' and, of course, those pensions and new cars for union officials.

For years the controversy had raged over this No.2 a/c and there had never been a satisfactory reply. Don Smith had been reported as denying any such PPL fund existed. Now, as I've mentioned, following complaints about its administration, the MMC had stepped in and all was revealed. The MMC found this money should have been paid to the recording musicians and determined this money shall be paid to those recording musicians who were on those records that had been broadcast over the years. Forced to defend themselves, the Executive Committee mysteriously found a piece of paper dated some time in 1946 which stated monies would be paid to the Musicians Union by the Phonographic Performance Fund for the general benefit of the music industry. I say that the piece of paper was found, but no one was ever allowed to see it, and there were plenty of requests. Copies of a 78 r.p.m. record were found stating (in the form of a promo for the PPL) money collected from broadcasts would be distributed to record companies, artists and those musicians who performed on the records. I repeat — *musicians who performed on the records*. As clear evidence as it was, such statements, although recorded, were classed as hearsay by the union and could not be considered as an acceptable argument.

Following the inquiry and ruling of the MMC, the union suddenly did an abrupt about turn and, disregarding all the controversy including a heated written exchange between the General Secretary and me in *The Musician* magazine, were making themselves out to be the great benefactors who could now distribute largess to all and sundry. As you might have gathered, some of us were beginning to think the only qualification that was needed to receive thousands of pounds from the union was to have an old Tandberg tape recorder or some such piece of equipment gathering dust under your bed or, at best, a White Label of some disbanded rehearsal group.

Realising the amount of work involved in the continued distribution of payments, which was one reason the union opted not to do it back in 1946, a separate organization was set up. Performing Artists' Media Rights Association (P@MRA) came into being in 1996. Not to lose their grip on the great deal of money involved, the General Secretary, Dennis Scard and another Executive Committee member, Johnny Patrick, were appointed 'advisers' to P@MRA. As can be expected with any new organization, rules were made and changed and changed again so the qualifications needed to be eligible for payments were becoming quite stringent.

I personally have had to write to record producers, musical directors, composers and artists, even to a top executive of Sony Music, to get verification of the work I did and I take this opportunity to thank them all for their cooperation. Way back in the late 'forties and early 'fifties all payments to musicians for recording work were paid out of petty cash. The money these worthy gentlemen made was considerably more than the average wage and it allowed them to purchase property and other blue chip investments — and good luck to them. Waking up to this loophole, the Inland Revenue ruled all payments must be registered and declared. Instead of taking the opportunity then to detail who was on what record, the union carried on as if no registration had been ordered and missed the golden opportunity to benefit the recording musician.

It took until 1973 when the dreaded Value Added Tax (VAT) was implemented for consent forms and other methods of registration to be introduced. All self-employed persons with an annual income exceeding a certain amount had to register for VAT. This included the majority of recording musicians so, at the end of every session, out would come the VAT Books and invoices were given to the fixer or whomever needed them. This was another opportunity the union missed to get details of 'who was on what record.'

Had we been told, every musician would have put the full details on his VAT invoice. It would only have meant a few more seconds work and the benefits (had they been explained) would have been fair and long-term compensation. But why should the Union change the status quo when it was doing all right for itself?

Another factor was that at that time, there still wasn't anyone in the union who was responsible for the recording musicians' interest. We were considered to be making enough money to look after ourselves. The bottom line of the PPL fund tragicomedy is that all those musicians who played on records in the 'sixties and 'seventies will never be fairly compensated. Not only is there insufficient data to back up any claims made by those musicians but also, after eight years, any unclaimed money is forwarded to the record companies.

The difficulty and effort needed to get one's name attached to a specific recording was daunting. To prove that I had recorded 'World without Love' with Peter Asher and Gordon Waller on electric 12 string, I had to contact Peter at his office as Senior Vice President of Sony Music

Entertainment. Peter was gracious enough to write a letter confirming my work on the recording. Below is just a fraction of some correspondence I had to enter into to get my name attached to 'Silhouettes,' a recording by Peter Noone and the Herman's Hermits. It is also evident how convoluted and misinformwhated is the listing of musicians:

> SILHOUETTES
> The track number 0000622408 is the same recording as track number 0007884398 yet my name does not appear on track number 0007884398. Further proof is found in an extract from the 1960s Shop Magazine with quotes from guitarist Keith Hopwood, one of the original Herman's Hermits.
>
> Thank you for your kind attention and please update your records.
>
> > Best wishes,
> > Vic Flick
>
> Quote from Shop Magazine:
> 'was EXTREMELY happy to hear back from original HERMITS guitarist KEITH HOPWOOD on this once he saw how much press our little series was generating…while he refused to get mixed up in the whole mess of what, when, where and why, he did offer a LITTLE bit of insight into some of the goings-on POST-PETER NOONE'
>
> 'Hi, Kent. Been away a few days, unable to access my mails, and have returned a pretty full box — and a big chunk from you! This thing has certainly generated some print hasn't it?
>
> Sorry, but I've no intention of becoming embroiled in a slanging match about who played on what. I'm sure Peter's list is more or less correct. Suffice to say we did not play on all our records, for whatever reason. Oh, and yes, it was Vic Flick who played on Silhouettes. And yes, I would have been a lot more unhappy about it all if it were my songs he was using the session guys on. — Keith Hopwood.'

In the United States the musicians were being well taken care of. Certainly forceful action had to be taken to get to such a position, but in the very early years of the recording business the American Federation of Musicians realised their members who were involved with recording needed their futures looked after. Vast sums were being made by artists, agents, managers and recording companies and it seemed only fair that musicians should benefit as well. Because of the AFofM's foresight, American musicians are doing very nicely with large pensions and many other benefits.

The top echelon of the British Musicians Union were often in discussion with and sometimes guests of the AFofM and were very aware of what could be done for their members. Again, nothing was done. Even if the actions taken by the AFofM had been suggested for implementation to the British Musicians' Union Executive Committee, such suggestions would have fallen on deaf ears. After all, following the exchanges I had had with the Executive Committee, there appeared to be little sympathy for those 'damned subversive reactionaries' amongst the committee's membership.

Coda

As of this writing, Judy and I have been married 47 years. It's a long time when one stops and thinks about it, but the time has gone by in a flash. We have always been looking for something new, something to test us and, believe me, we have been sorely tested without even trying. We had been married for about 25 years when we both discovered our separate desires to be in the United States of America.

At the tender age of six I left home to go to America to be a cowboy. My mother said she watched me as I walked toward the end of our street. I had made myself a sandwich for the journey, and putting some clothing in a leather bag, headed out to the New World. A few hundred yards down the street, my footsteps faltered, I stopped and turned, and walked slowly back to the house. Mission unaccomplished, but at least I had made a start.

The local Shrewsbury newspaper had a contest asking for letters from children about their futures. Judy had entered a letter when she was 11 years old about her wanting to be a cowgirl in America. Judy wrote of the romance and the open spaces of that mysterious and wonderful place, America, and how she wanted to be part of it. Of course, all these dreams were prompted by visits to the local cinema where the goodies and the baddies battled it out on the Lone Prairie, and Judy could lose herself in the romantic liaisons between cowboy and the rancher's daughter. Back in the 1950s it was cowboys and Indians, whooping and shooting across the silver screen in a black-and-white 45-minute 'B' film. Now things are different and there is rarely a good cowboy and Indian film to be seen.

As mentioned earlier, in 1974 I was asked by percussionist Jock Cummings to join his 'celebrity' band on a three-week cruise to the Caribbean and the East Coast of America. I wasn't his first choice, as guitarist Dick Abel had decided to paint his house instead of working the cruise, but you have to grab opportunities when they are presented! Our first stop was in the Port of Fort Lauderdale, Florida. I had a shopping list of things to buy in America: a Fender Rhodes Electric piano for

Les Reed, a Martin D28 for me and other smaller items for friends and relatives. We left the ship and waited for a taxi. It is amazing how just one person can be more of an ambassador for a country than a whole Government department. The cab driver was wonderful. He took us to Sea World and the Music Store and Publix Supermarket and a restaurant for hamburgers, and was always waiting when we needed him. I was concerned we were taking business from him but he was adamant that we were happy and that we did what we wanted to do. Strolling along the beach at Fort Lauderdale, Judy and I looked at each other and said, 'We want some of this.'

And so began our journey to the States.

With more musicians having their own project studios and the record companies being more careful with their money, and television using more and more pre-recorded music, the session scene was starting to cool down by the end of the 'seventies. The indications were that things would not improve. We are only here once and it's a big world, let's go see it.

By the beginning of the 'eighties, plans were made for the big move for Judy, Jayne, Kevin and I to move to America.

Now, that's another book!

Geoff Leonard
imbd.com

Robert Z. Rush D.C.
Musician, Journalist

Wes Britton
Author, *www,spywise.net*

Matt Sherman
www.commanderbond.net

My thanks to the above for their advice and encouragement.

Vic Flick

Equipment

Fender Stratocaster #65810
Fender Stratocaster
Fender Squire
Martin D28
Gibson L7C
Vox Electric 12 String
Epiphone 12 String
Fender Precision Bass
Burns Six String Bass
Gibson Mastertone Banjo
Fender Vibrolux Amplifier 1962

Index

A'Hern, Pete 164
Addey, Malcolm 152
AIR London Studios 76
AIR Lyndhurst 76
Andrews, Chris 74, 143
Anka, Paul 19, 20, 172
Arnold, David 129
Arthey, Johnny 100
Asher, Peter 177
Aynsworth, Alan 56, 90, 104, 163

Bacharach, Burt 57
Barry Sisters 27
Barry, John 5, 19, 20-26
Bassey, Shirley 95, 137, 138
Beadle, Len 27
Beatles, The 76, 131-133, 137
Bell, Billy 57
Bell, Tim 115
Bellson, Louis 101
Bennett, Brian 148
Benson, Harry 152
Berry, Dave 60, 146
Bigden, Alf 59
Birkin, Jayne 88, 142
Black is Black 65
Black, Cilla 137
Black, Don 128
Blackburn, Tony 97
Blackwell, Charles 60, 83, 146
Blue Boar Cafeteria 47
Bond, James 19, 65, 87, 121, 122, 138
Botkin Jnr, .Perry 56, 57

Bowen, Greg 157
Boyce, Denny 119
Brennan, Rose 54
Britton, Wes 183
Brosnan, Pierce 129
Brown, Joe 149
Burgess, John 32
Butler, Gerry 29
Butlins Holiday Camps 15, 16, 117, 146

Cameron, John 58, 59
Cannes 73
Carr, Bobby 33
Carr, Tony 59
Cattini, Clem 132
CBS 77, 146
Chappell's Recording Studio 77
Clapton, Eric 126
Clark, Les 15
Clark, Petula 143
Clarke, Frank 152
Cobham, Billy 100
Coffee Bar, 2Is 63, 147
Cogan, Alma 141
Coleman, John 105
Connery, Sean 129
Conti, Bill 129
Cooper, Ray 41, 128
Cort, Bob 18, 19
Costello, Elvis 54
Coulan, Roger 132
Coulter, Phil 164
Crosby, Bing 167

CTS Recording Studios 125
Cummings, Jock 115
Curtis, Chris 141

Dale, Syd 107
Dalton, Timothy 129
Daly, Bryan 25, 29, 66, 91, 93, 103, 143, 155, 165
Davis Jnr, Sammy 140
Day, Jill 35
Dean, John 59, 95, 108
Decca Radar 12
Decca Recording Studios 64, 65, 84, 125
Dee, Simon 167
DeMato, Tony 70
Denham Film Studios 65, 105, 126
Dig This 23
Distel, Sacha 55
Dizley, Diz 19
Donovan 145
Douglas, Craig 73
Drumbeat 22, 25-29,

Eager, Vince 27, 49
Eddy, Duane 32
Embassy Records 77
EMI Studios 31, 32,

Faith, Adam 23, 27, 46, 53, 83, 143
Farlow, Tal 12
Firman, Alec 150
Flick, Mick 109
Flowers, Herbie 132
Ford, Eric 91, 95, 103
Fry, Tristan 173
Fury, Billy 49

Gainesboro, Serge 142
Gentry, Bobby 58
Geraldo 77
Gerhardt, Chuck 157
Gilbert, Tony 167
Gillespie, Frank 119

Gordeno, Peter 27
Gradwell, Chris 173
Grant, Keith 69, 70, 85, 96
Green, Colin 155
Green, Ron 29
Greenslade, Arthur 94, 143, 162
Gretton, Larry 54
Grey, Steve 132
Grob, Alex 79
Guest, Reg 99

Habig, Joe 157
Hall, Jim 12
Hamlisch, Marvin 142
Hardy, Francoise 142
Harris, Johnny 140
Harris, Max 115, 156, 167, 169
Harris, Richard 12
Harwood, Dickie 22
Hawksworth, Johnny 158
Hayward, Justin 170
Hazelby, Brian 38
Hazlehurst, Ronnie 155
Heath, Ted 98, 106, 144, 158
Hewson, Richard 131
Hicks, Clive 57, 60, 66, 148
Hiseman, Jon 29
Honeywell, Don 154
Hopkins, Mary 83
Hopkins, Nicky 83
Hopwood, Keith 178
Horrox, Frank 106
Humperdink, Engelbert 37, 65, 84, 94, 147
Hunter, Len 29
Hurdle, Les 90, 173

IBC Studios 76, 89

Jackson, Jack 22
Jennings Music 22, 125, 147
Jennings, George 18
Jones, Jack 60

INDEX

Jones, Tom 37, 60, 64, 84, 145

Kamen, Michael 126, 129
Katz, Charlie 95, 150, 152
Katz, David 170
Keating, Johnny 98
Keel, Howard 167
Kelly, Keith 21, 22
Kerr, Anita 79
Kershaw, Martin 100
King Brothers, The 46
King, Dennis (Sax) 26, 34
Kirchin, Basil 48, 105
Kish, George 149

Lang, Don 46, 50
Lawless, Jim 101, 108, 132, 164
Lazenby, George 129
Leander, Mike 154
Lee, Jackie 27
LeGrand, .Michel 84
Leonard, Geoff 183
Leper, Bob 140
Levy's Studios 77
Leyton, John 64
Littlewood, Yvonne 23
Longine Company 155
Loss, Joe 41, 54
Lulu 83
Lusher, Don 157
Lyttleton, Trevor 174

Mancini, Henry 65, 93, 156
Manhattan Transfer 168
Margo, Syd 150, 152
Martin, Bill 164
Martin, Sir George 81, 129, 132
Martin, Lee (Bostick) 37
Marvin, Hank 146, 147
Mason, Barry 37, 97
Mason, Glen 22
McCartney, Paul 131
McGowan, Kathy 144

McGrath, Nuggy 36
McKuen, Rod 85, 86, 94
McManus, Ross 54
Meek, Joe 63, 72, 152
Midgley, Bobby 94
Miller, Mrs. 140
Miller, Bob 23, 27, 47, 53
Milligan, .Spike 59, 60
Mills, Gordon 64, 84
Minelli, Liza 170, 171
Mitchell, Malcolm 79
Mitchum, Robert 166
Mojo Magazine 121
Monkhouse, Bob 79
Monshin, Bernard 150
Moore, Bobby 90
Moore, Roger 129, 138
Moretti, Joe 88, 89, 103, 142
Morgan, Pete 164
Morley, Angela 70, 156
Morris, Stewart 22, 23, 28, 29
Most, Mickie 82, 83
Mudlarks, The 48
Musicians' Union 100, 108, 124, 151, 173

Neve Desks 72
Newell, Norman 32
Newley, Anthony 65, 90, 91
Noone, Peter 178
Norman, Monty 121, 124

O'Sullivan, Gilbert 84
Oh Boy 22, 164
Olaf, Peter 72, 142
Old Bailey, The 121, 124
Olympic Sound Studios 69, 71, 76, 84, 86, 96, 140

Page, Jimmy 60, 83, 103, 145, 147, 155
Page, Lisa 35
Paine, Cy 79
Paramour, Norrie 18
Parkinson, Michael 164, 166

Parnes, Larry 48
Pass, Joe 12
Patrick, John 177
Pearson, Johnny 95, 97, 167, 170
Peter and Gordon 83, 159
Peters, Mike 26, 33
Phillips Studio 72, 73, 74, 99, 165
Price, Ronnie 143, 160, 161, 163
Prickett, Ray 74, 149
Proctor, Judd 57, 103
PYE Studios 58, 74, 142, 149

Raindrops, The 27, 56
Raymond, Ivor 65, 101, 102
Readers Digest 57, 93, 106
Reed OBE, Les 16, 22, 29, 43, 50, 97
Reeves, Jim 101, 102
Regent Sound Studios 63
Rich, Buddy 139
Richard, Cliff 18, 146
Richards, John 65, 68, 93
Richmond, Dave 66, 89, 95, 108, 157, 171
Riddle, Nelson 74, 157
Ridley, Wally 97, 98
Rock & Roll Hall of Fame 19, 125
Roderick, Stan 70
Rogers, Clodagh 36
Rogers, Louis 36
Rolling Stones, The 52, 83, 117
Rosa, Lita 144
Ross, Mike 77
Rowe, Dick 73, 132
Royal Variety 54
Rush, Bob 8, 183
Russell, Ray 147

Salmon, Kenny 43, 159
Samwell, Sammy 18
Sanderson, Tommy 99
Sands, Sylvia 27, 29
Sax, Sid 125, 152
Scard, Dennis 177
Schroeder, John 97

Shadows, The 52
Shaw, Roland 125, 156
Shaw, Sandie 74, 143, 144
Shear, Ernie 57, 80, 91
Sherman, Matt 183
Shorey, Len 163
Sinatra, Frank 74, 138
Sinatra, Nancy 140
Small, Millie 144
Smart, Harold 159
Smith, Don 173, 174, 175
Spain, Nancy 49
Spedding, Chris 149
Springfield, Dusty 45, 74, 139, 142, 149
Squadronaires 47
Squires, Dorothy 138, 139
Staff, Freddy 115
Stead, Jimmy 26, 33
Stern, Isaac 171
Stewart, James 164
Stoneham, Harry 164, 167
Stott, Wally 69
Streisand, Barbara 84, 85
Stringbeat 31, 32, 161
Sullivan, Big Jim 69, 92, 146, 148
Sullivan, Peter 84
Summer, Donna 90
Sykora, Ken 19

Tarago, Renata 88
Taylor, Ted 51, 161
Taylor, Eve 21, 22, 23, 83, 143
Temple, Nat 47
Thatcher, Les 154
Thorne, Ken 98, 156
Thrillington 131
Timperly, John 78
Tiomkin, Dimitri 65
Tomlinson, Eric 65, 126
Top Rank Records 64, 73
Tornados, The 64, 160
Townsend, Cliff 115
Trident Studios 79, 115
Twinkle 164

Vandyke, Les 27
Verral, Ronnie 164

Walker Bothers, The 27
Waller, Gordon 177
Walsh, Terry 155
Watkins, Derek 157
Watts, Charlie 117
Weedon, Bert 27
Weighell, Alan 54, 149
Welch, Bruce 147
White, Andy 29, 132
Whittaker, David 106

Wilde, Marty 48, 52, 105
Williams, Danny 27
Willox, Roy 100, 157
Wimbledon Palaise 51
Winston, Eric 16, 18, 120
Wirtz, Mark 82
Woodman, Kenny 74, 143
Worth, Johnny 27
Wright, Dougie 26, 29, 34, 41, 41, 43, 51

Young, Roy 25, 26

Printed in Great Britain
by Amazon